British Railwa
Modernisation-Era
DMUs

Evan Green-Hughes

The
· Transport ·
Treasury

© Images and design: The Transport Treasury 2021. Text Evan Green-Hughes

ISBN 978-1-913251-16-1

First Published in 2021 by Transport Treasury Publishing Ltd. 16 Highworth Close, High Wycombe, HP13 7PJ

www.ttpublishing.co.uk

Printed in the UK by Henry Ling Limited, at the Dorset Press, Dorchester. DT1 1HD.

Contents

Front Cover: One of the most numerous types of DMU were the suburban classes, which were all to the same basic design. The Class 117s were built by Pressed Steel and one of these is seen in original condition and original plain green livery speeding through High Wycombe with a train bound for Aylesbury.

Frontispiece: Because BR's own workshops could not cope with the demand many DMUs were built by outside contractors. Here a Cravens-built Class 105 works an Aberdeen-Ballater service on May 19th 1959 and crosses the unique battery-powered unit at Park Station, Drumoak.

Opposite: By the end of the 1950s the advantages of having purpose-built accommodation had become obvious. One of the depots to benefit from this was Neville Hill in Leeds where part of the former steam site was rebuilt to house diesel multiple units, with the new facilities opening to much fanfare in June 1960. Here a Class 111 unit in original condition breaks the ceremonial barrier to declare the new building well and truly open

Rear Cover: Although it became practice to use a traditional oil tail lamp, there was a plan to use plastic red discs inserted in the marker lights as tail lights. Here the proposed system is demonstrated, presumably in a posed shot perhaps for the members of the press.

Introduction

Diesel Multiple Units, or DMUs for short, are today a dominant part of the railway scene with their popularity being down to their low running costs, high utilisation and operational flexibility.

However, 70 years ago, things were quite different with local and urban transit mostly in the hands of trains made up of steam engines and separate coaches. Such trains cost a lot of money to run and in the depression years after World War Two were one of the reasons that the British railway network was haemorrhaging money, leading to a funding crisis that has to some extent dogged the railways ever since. Trains powered by internal-combustion engines offered the possibility of cutting those costs with several railways building prototypes in the early years of the 20th century. Most of these were single-car vehicles with petrol engines and electric transmission which offered modest performance and capacity, with the overriding issue being the power that was available from the then-available engines.

It wasn't until 1933 that a really successful railcar was built, this being constructed as a joint project between the Great Western Railway, Hardy Motors and AEC, and this was to prove the forerunner of a very successful class of 38 vehicles, which as well as being operated on a huge variety of services were also demonstrated in other areas of the country. By this time diesel engines were in use, with some of the cars being organised in such a fashion as they were single-ended and coupled back to back so as to form two-car sets.

One of the most influential of the pre-war designs which laid out many of the mechanical foundations of the first-generation units were the 38 Great Western Railway railcars, which were built between 1934 and 1942. Although the majority were single cars, some were built as two-car units. All established the principle of using AEC engines coupled with epicyclic gearboxes and were very successful in traffic. Earlier examples had bodies by Park Royal and Gloucester Railway Carriage Works, with one of these being GRCW-built no 15, which is seen here between duties at Birmingham Snow Hill on November 25 1957 alongside a Class 117 suburban unit. No 15, by then re-numbered W15W, was equipped with two AEC 130hp engines and had more rounded bodywork, compared to later builds.

Introduction

Although diesels were coming into widespread use by this time, the majority of British trains were still powered by steam and this continued to be the case until the early 1950s when the newly-nationalised British Railways set up the Lightweight Trains Committee which was tasked with the job of finding how to dramatically cut the costs of working branch and secondary lines. Members travelled extensively and examined various diesel options which had been put into service, particularly in Germany and France, but they also went to Ireland where a fleet of successful diesel railcars had been developed which shared many mechanical components with the GWR's units and which had slashed running costs on the services that they operated. Consideration was also given to other options, too, including the use of 'Sentinel' type steam engines and the development of a modern 'push-pull' train-set which would have used an updated 2-6-2 tank engine for motive power.

In the end the committee came down in favour of a two-car diesel multiple unit, powered by diesel engines, and with a driving position at each end. Unfortunately, at that time the only engines available could only provide 125hp, which was judged to be insufficient for the new trains to perform to the current timetables. A radical answer was required and this came from the designers at Derby Carriage Works who came up with the idea of constructing the new trains from aluminium, thus saving about five tons per carriage.

The first of the new trains, which from then on have always been known as 'Derby Lightweights', was outshopped in 1954, with the initial batch being allocated to services between Leeds, Bradford and Harrogate. Due to the hilly nature of the route both coaches were powered and each had two engines, giving 500hp for a complete set. Uniquely for these eight sets Lysholm Smith transmission was used, instead of the Wilson gearboxes that had been used in Ireland.

Several batches of a slightly revised design then followed, with one powered and one unpowered car per two-car set. By now 150hp engines were available from AEC and these were used along with Wilson gearboxes, which necessitated changes to the electrical coupling arrangements, rendering the original eight sets unable to work with any others. Several areas received these trains, including West Cumberland, East Anglia, Lincolnshire and North Wales.

By this time, it was becoming obvious that BR's own works could not produce enough of these trains to satisfy the demand and so what was called 'the trade' was invited to submit tenders for similar designs. The first company to be successful was Metropolitan-Cammell of Birmingham, whose distinctive design first appeared in 1955. Mechanically it was very similar to the Derby product but its styling was very different, and it was much heavier due to its mainly steel construction. Despite this the earliest batches of the 'Met-Cam' cars are often referred to as 'lightweights'.

Several other manufacturers also obtained orders, in some cases for hundreds of vehicles, and these included large numbers for the Birmingham Railway Carriage and Wagon Company, Pressed Steel and the Gloucester Carriage and Wagon Company. Also successful were smaller manufacturers some of whom, such as D. Wickham of Ware, built only a handful of units.

The year 1956 saw the introduction of the first inter-urban DMU sets, which were intended for the Edinburgh-Glasgow route, and these were produced by Swindon works to the general style of a Mark One coach, although with revised underframe arrangements. Further sets to this general design, though revised, appeared later.

Suburban travellers were provided with a design specially made for short journeys which featured a longer underframe and more bodyside doors. The general specification for these was drawn up at Derby but examples were also built by Pressed Steel and Gloucester with sets mostly being of three or four coaches but with two batches of single cars being built for the most lightly-used services.

The final development was for longer distance services, for the Trans-Pennine route and for the Western Region, with again Swindon works taking a leading role.

British Railways' DMU fleet eventually totalled more than 4,600 vehicles with all being built within six years of the first, a remarkable achievement. Unfortunately, no one had expected the cuts that came in the following decade with the result that many units, particularly from the smaller classes, were sent to the cutters' torch before 1970. The rest survived mainly until the mid-1980s when large numbers of 'Pacers' and 'Sprinters' arrived for service. First to go were those cars that had been insulated with deadly blue asbestos, while the bulk of the rest went in the mid-1990s. Some hung on until December 2003 but after that there were only a couple of single cars at work on the Aylesbury to Princes Risborough branch and these finally went in 2019.

Evan Green-Hughes, 2021.

Chapter One
The Early Diesel Units

Before the advent of conventional first-generation DMUs there had been a number of experiments with diesel trains. Several of these, such as those operated by the North Eastern Railway, had electric transmission, which takes them outside the scope of this book. There were, however, some railcars and multiple units which used diesel engines and mechanical transmission, some of which led directly to the development of the diesel multiple unit with which we were to become familiar.

Above: The GWR introduced a refined and updated version of the railcar shown on the previous page in 1940 which was more angular in appearance. Again equipped with AEC engines, these vehicles were built by the GWR itself at its Swindon works and were turned out in chocolate and cream livery. Following nationalisation these cars began to appear in carmine and cream coaching stock colours, and it is this livery that is worn by W20W at Ironbridge and Broseley Station in 1960. This station was on the Severn Valley line north of Bridgnorth and was closed on September 9 1963, the site now being occupied by a car park.

Opposite top: Following nationalisation there was a great deal of interest in the Great Western cars and the newly-formed British Railways arranged for a number of trials to be conducted in various parts of the country using them. One such trial was in Yorkshire in 1952 where W20W was put to work on services between Bradford and Harrogate, this was one of the routes that was the first to receive first-generation units when they began to be introduced from 1954 onwards. For some reason at this time the car was running with part of its lower skirts removed, which gives a clearer view than normal of the layout of the engines, gearboxes and final drives. Bradford Exchange Station was originally a joint venture between the Lancashire and Yorkshire Railway and the Great Northern and opened in 1850. It lasted until 1973 when it was replaced by the new Interchange Station, which is a few hundred yards to the south.

Opposite bottom: In their final years the Great Western railcars received mid-Brunswick green livery, which was the darker of British Railways' two multiple unit liveries. By this time the fleet was employed on duties on minor branch lines, one of which was the Severn Valley route from Kidderminster through Bewdley. What is thought to be W31W calls at Bewdley Station on what is now the heritage Severn Valley Railway while wearing this later livery, which includes the 'speed whiskers' more normally associated with later units. Bewdley Station opened in 1862 and was one of the main stations on the West Midland Railway's Hartlebury to Shrewsbury route. Network services lasted until 1970, after which the preservationists took over.

Opposite top: Within this final batch of vehicles was one railcar intended for parcels use only, with this being numbered W34W and, in BR days, turned out in crimson coaching stock colours. This was the second parcels car and like its earlier sister it had no windows or passenger seats. Three large sliding doors were provided on each side to facilitate the loading of parcels and goods. This car was deployed between Reading and London where its duties included a run to Kensington to pick up consignments of Lyons cakes. By this time conventional vacuum brakes were being fitted to these railcars in place of the automotive-style vacuum over hydraulic system originally fitted to the early cars. W34W is seen at Westbourne Bridge near Paddington station on March 30 1957.

Opposite bottom: The London Midland and Scottish Railway also operated a number of diesel-mechanical units, though in this case they were four-wheelers, being introduced into service in June 1934. Equipped with a Leyland 95hp engine and Lysholm-Smith transmission (later to appear on the first DMUs proper) these three vehicles had seats for 40 people. Trials took place in February 1934 between Preston and Carlisle with the units initially allocated to Blackburn shed. During the war two were sent to Hamilton In Scotland, and were joined by the fourth in 1949. By then only one was in use, the rest providing spares. Here the first one of the batch, 29950, is seen at the terminus of the Coalburn branch in South Lanarkshire on June 28 1948. All were withdrawn in 1951.

Above; The next development in this area took place in 1953 when Associated Commercial Vehicles produced three vehicles initially as a private venture in response to a perceived demand for such vehicles on lines where it was desired to reduce operating costs and overheads. These had a body by Park Royal and underframe and mechanicals by AEC. Following early trials these found a home on the St Albans to Watford line. This is the first car built, no 1, which later became M79740. Although marshalled as a three-car set, the end cars, which were both powered, had a driving cab at each end and therefore these vehicles could be used singly or in two or three-car formation.

This page: The first set, which can easily be identified due to its droplight windows, was trialled extensively around the network, being based initially at Neasden for work out of Marylebone station. It then worked for a time on the Epping to Ongar branch before being deployed on other services in the London area. After a visit to Scotland and Hull the train spent 12 days in Birmingham in early September 1953 before moving on again. It is seen here in the company of BR 'standard' class 2-6-2 tank 82001 at Birmingham Moor Street during its West Midlands visit. (Mike Hughes)

Opposite bottom; The prototype set travelled widely in its first couple of years and was used extensively for publicity as well as for tests. Some of the photographs were taken at Marylebone station before the unit went into public service, and during this period the set worked a few trains in the immediate area. It is seen here at West Ruislip Station in original condition and livery. These three coaches differed from later ones in that they had a skirt or valance over the wheels and extending from the lower bodywork. West Ruislip was opened in April 1906 as a joint station constructed by the Great Western and the Great Central as part of a plan to provide an alternative route for GC trains into London while avoiding the tracks of the Metropolitan Railway.

Right: The interior of the ACV/BUT vehicle was very sparse by railway standards and, given its Park Royal parentage, it's not surprising that it bore more resemblance to the interior of a bus than a train. The driver sat in a half-cab which was the original arrangement that was proposed for the first-generation DMUs where his every action came under intense scrutiny from the passengers. On October 8 1953 the railcar is in motion at Buttlesbridge in Essex during tests. The droplight windows would suggest that this is the interior of one of the two power cars from the prototype batch.

Top: In January 1955 the three-car set was purchased by British Railways, which had also ordered a further set as well as a spare power car. A third three-car set was added in 1957. These later vehicles can easily be identified by their sliding window lights and lack of skirts round the lower body. Like the earlier vehicles they were provided with AEC 125hp engines and epicyclic gearboxes but unlike the first batch they were delivered in BR green livery, into which scheme the earlier vehicles were soon painted. The differences are readily apparent in this shot of M79744 which was one of the power cars from the second set, but which was often used singly. On one of its regular duties, which commenced in July 1955, it stands in the bay at Watford Junction while waiting to perform a service to St Albans.

Bottom: Another view of one of the later power cars, which is seen at Watford North, which was the first station on the St Albans Branch, and is located around three quarters of a mile North East of Watford Junction. The branch was opened in 1858 by the London and North Western but this station did not open until 1910, then being named Callowland. It was renamed in 1927 but suffered declining patronage, along with the rest of the line, and was threatened with closure. Today the whole line is electrified and carries more than 100,000 passengers each year.

Chapter Two

The Lightweights

In the early 1950s British Railways' 'Lightweight Trains Committee', following extensive deliberation, recommended that diesel multiple units were to be the preferred traction for local and suburban services.

Derby Works was entrusted with producing the required units, utilising features from the former GWR vehicles and those already in service in Ireland. A £500,000 pilot scheme in the Leeds-Bradford area was followed up with a more extensive deployment of units in Cumberland, East Anglia, North Wales and

Lincolnshire. The Derby works products were soon joined by vehicles built by Metropolitan-Cammell of Birmingham, which while mechanically similar were of completely different body design. These sets were all very successful but were not electrically compatible with those built later on, and thus were early candidates for withdrawal following a reduced requirement for trains after the Beeching cuts.

The initial order was for eight sets, which can readily be identified from later builds by the lack of a lower centre marker light and the jumper cable arrangement. Two Leyland 125hp engines were fitted to each car, and Leyland Lysholm Smith pre-selector gearboxes were used. Extensive use was made of aluminium alloy in construction with sections being rivetted together, with the resulting coaches costing around £5,000 more each than would have a conventional steel vehicle. However, due to the limited horsepower available, weight saving was considered to be a great priority. The first test run took place on April 12 1954 from Derby to Leicester and return, with other runs following, some of which were not without incident. Here one of the first units is in trouble while on a test run up the Melbourne Branch in Derbyshire, and which was at that time still open for freight and test train purposes.

Above: Another photograph taken at Melbourne shows the prototype Driving Motor Brake E79000 posed for photographs. The up-to-date modern image which the official photograph was intended to portray is rather spoilt by the grubby oil tail lamp which someone has put on the vehicle end ready for the return trip to Derby. Only nine years before this photograph was taken Melbourne was part of the Melbourne Military Railway, as the branch had been taken over by the War Department during World War II, but it was returned to civilian use in 1945, finally closing as a freight-only route in 1980. Passenger services ceased as early as 1930.

Opposite top: Introduction of the new trains took place on June 14 1954, with them being deployed on routes between Leeds Central and Bradford Exchange stations, as well as to Harrogate. The eight sets were diagrammed to cover 309,000 miles a week and replaced a large number of steam engines and carriages. Their appearance in West Yorkshire caused a great deal of interest amongst the travelling public, with a rise in passenger numbers being reported immediately. In fact, after seven years of DMU operation four times as many people were using the route as had been in the latter days of steam. At Leeds Central the local train to Bradford attracts much attention from the travelling public.

Opposite bottom: At the time of the introduction of diesel multiple units the railways were very run down, and this is well-exhibited in this scene at Bradford Exchange station where one of the early batch of Derby Lightweight units sets off on its journey to Leeds. Driving Motor Composite E79501 was the second one built and like all vehicles in this batch was adorned with the British Railways cycling lion emblem, more normally seen on locomotives. Unusually this batch had the motif on both the power and the trailer cars, while later ones had a transfer only on the power car. As built the West Riding cars had huge front windows, but later it was found necessary to fit them with strengthening bars.

The Lightweights

Opposite top: The ultra-modern DMUs did not stay very clean for very long, and soon acquired the same coating of filth which adorned everything else on the railways at that time. Here one of the 'West Riding' sets leaves Leeds Central station on yet another of its runs to Bradford Exchange. Leeds Central was opened as a joint station by four different companies in 1854 and lasted until 1967, when its services were transferred to Leeds City Station. The 'West Riding' sets did not live to see even this closure, as withdrawal took place in 1964, when they were only ten years old, largely as a result of their non-standard transmission and coupling arrangements.

Opposite bottom: The first two batches of 'Lightweights' had a large window between the guard's van and the first vestibule which served a small compartment with nine seats in it. This meant that the guard's van was unusually small so that in the event only the first two batches of these units had this arrangement. The second unit built, headed by Driving Motor Brake E79001, is pictured on one of its first runs to Harrogate. The unique electrical jumpers are clearly seen in this view, and these were only fitted to the first eight sets. No lower central marker light was fitted to this batch and instead a lamp iron was supplied, on which could be mounted a conventional oil lamp of the period.

Above: The second area selected as a pilot scheme for the new units was West Cumberland, and in particular lines from Whitehaven to Carlisle, Penrith to Carlisle and the former Cockermouth, Keswick and Penrith east-west route. Thirteen sets were constructed, being first introduced into service from November 1954 and their introduction was marked with an increase in service frequency and faster end to end times. In the first 12 months of the new service passenger numbers rose from 59,000 per year to 91,600. Seen while working the 1020 Penrith to Workington service just before departure on May 18 1955 is Driving Motor Brake M79608.

Above: Later in their lives the 'West Cumberland' lightweights spread their wings a little and could often be seen, as here, further afield at places such as Preston. Although produced only months after the West Riding sets there were numerous differences between this and the previous batch, in particular the use of Wilson epicyclic gearboxes and a different form of control, which resulted in a revision to the jumper cable arrangements. The engines used were of BUT (AEC) manufacture and were used in place of Leylands as they could offer 150hp instead of 125hp while the final drives this time came from AEC, rather than Walker Brothers. Due to previous problems with the windscreens, strengthening bars were provided behind them, while bars were provided over the droplights due to limited clearances on the old Maryport and Carlisle system. Only the motor brake was powered, while the second car was a driving trailer, and it is one of these, M79607, which is seen here in early 1968 by which time some vehicles had received blue livery while others had gained full yellow ends.

Opposite bottom: There were more changes on subsequent batches of 'Derby Lightweights', although from then on all followed the same basic pattern. Most noticeable was the alteration in the windscreen arrangement with the large glass screens being broken up into two panels each so that a proper strengthening bar could be supplied. This in turn led to changes to the windscreen wiper arrangement, with two wipers being provided on the strengthening panel instead of only one mounted to the side. Batches were supplied for use in Lincolnshire, East Anglia, North Wales, Newcastle, Birmingham and Manchester. Here two two-car sets working in multiple are seen at Castle Bromwich station en route to Birmingham New Street.

Top: One of the features of the Derby Lightweights which proved to be universally popular was the view through the cab, enabling passengers to see the railway in front of them. This was particularly appreciated in the Lake District, but was equally as popular in built-up areas. Here a youngster is fascinated by the road ahead and the work of the driver. As can be seen the Derby Lightweights had a rather expensive high-backed seating arrangement, which was dropped in favour of 'bus type' seats when the later version, better known as Class 108, came out.

Middle: The Derby Lightweights arrived on a railway that had suffered under investment for many years, and in many locations had not changed at all since the day of opening. Despite the ultra-modern, for the time, diesel train, Penrith Station was still a dark and dismal place and conditions on this and other stations did little to attract the traveller. The marker lights on DMUs were initially used in the same way as steam locomotive oil headcode lamps, with the sequence of lights illuminated indicating what class of train was being operated. In this case the single light above the windows indicates that a stopping passenger train is being worked.

Above: 'Derby Lightweights' were extensively used in North Wales and covered many lines, such as those to Amlwch and Caernarfon, which have subsequently closed. Along with other classes of unit the 'Lightweights' soon acquired 'speed whiskers' as an aid to them being seen by track workers, they also were given the yellow diamond coupling code as their electrical system was not compatible with later-built units, and this symbol can clearly be seen just above each buffer. This pair of units, which include Driving Motor M79128 and Driving Trailer M79657, is calling at Llanfair station on Anglesey on July 20 1958. The station opened in August 1848, and still exists today situated on the main line to Holyhead although as a tourist gimmick, it is known as Llanfair PG, which in its full form is the longest station name in the country.

Opposite bottom: During the construction of the 'Derby Lightweights' an extra pair of bodyshells were constructed but not fitted with power equipment. They were then taken to Cowlairs works in Glasgow where they were fitted out as a battery-electric two-car set, which was then put to work on the Aberdeen to Ballater line. Numbered Sc79998 and Sc79999 this set was recharged using hydro-electric power. Introduced to service in 1958 it only lasted for four years but survived as a departmental vehicle and still exists today, at the Royal Deeside heritage line. This set can easily be identified by its lack of jumper cables, sockets or vacuum pipes; it was in fact unique amongst first-generation units in being air braked. It is seen here in Mayoral company when new at Ballater.

The Lightweights

Thirteen two-car 'Derby Lightweight' sets were provided for the Lincolnshire scheme and it was estimated that their introduction would save around £146,000 a year in operating costs. They were to the same basic pattern as the Cumberland sets, but had a larger guard's van, leading to a slight change in the bodyside design. One of these sets, made up of Driving Motor Brake E79035 and Driving Trailer E79251, calls at Mundesley-on-Sea with a Norwich-bound train on April 15 1956. As delivered the front ends were devoid of either speed whiskers or yellow warning panels.

Opposite top: Cavendish Station, on the Stour Valley Railway in East Anglia, was opened in 1865 but closed under the Beeching Axe in 1967. It was typical of the village stations which the Derby Lightweights served so well. Here a two-car set awaits the single line tablet while on a working to Sudbury. Today only the crossing keeper's house and a short section of platform are still in existence.

Opposite bottom: Before long it became obvious to the authorities that British Railways' own workshops would not have the capacity to build the number of diesel units that the operating department required and in consequence the decision was taken to ask what was described as 'the trade' to tender for the construction of some of them. The first manufacturer to be successful in obtaining some of this work was Metropolitan-Cammell of Birmingham, which produced a unit completely compatible with the Derby product mechanically but very different aesthetically. Both versions are seen here side by side at Norwich depot in 1958.

Above: The Metro-Cammell two-car DMU was very different from the Derby product, being made of steel and having a completely different body style, the design of which was finalised without reference to British Railways. This featured much smaller windows and a more raked-back front end. The first batch of these units went to the East Lancashire lines but then 29 sets were provided to work alongside the Derby Lightweights in East Anglia. One of these is seen at Haughley Station in Suffolk on May 3 1958 while working a stopping train bound for Ipswich. Haughley closed in January 1967 as part of the Beeching cuts which decimated the railway network of East Anglia.

Opposite: Two Metro-Cammell sets were loaned to the Scottish Region in April 1956 for around three months to see if they were suitable for services in the region. One of these, consisting of Driving Motor Brake E79055 and Driving Trailer E79271, was put to work on Gleneagles, Crieff and Comrie services and is seen at Muthill Station with the Driving Trailer leading. The picture will have been taken between June, when the experimental service commenced, and the end of July when this unit was transferred to Leith. Both sets were back in East Anglia by the September after having been warmly received in Scotland, with their visit leading to the early introduction of other classes of unit north of the Border. The trials did not, however, lead to salvation for Muthill station, which closed in 1964.

Above: The Scottish trials attracted a lot of attention from the local population, as can be seen here on June 21 1956 when the same set calls at Comrie Station, this time with the Driving Motor Brake leading. These early Metro-Cammell units can easily be identified as they have a prominent skirt fitted under the bufferbeam and four jumper sockets just under the cab windows. As built the actual jumper cables were stored in the cab and were only brought out when needed. These units lasted only until the beginning of 1969 when they were withdrawn wholesale due to the closure of most of the routes that they served, and to the non-standard nature of their 'yellow diamond' electrical system.

Above: The Metro-Cammell cars are often referred to as 'lightweights', though they were in fact five tons each car heavier than the Derby product, but performance was to the required standard due to the use of 150hp engines. They were delivered with a unique style of lining which featured three stripes, with the London Midland Region sets having 'speed whiskers' but the Eastern Region ones initially being without. The LM cars were often used on excursion work at the weekends in their early years, with runs to North Wales being particularly popular. Here three two-car sets are seen at an unknown location working such a service.

Opposite top: British Railways tried hard to get Metro-Cammell to change the design of their units, to bring them more into line with the Derby product. They were particularly concerned about the smaller windows, and the large corner pillars to the cab, but by the time the issue was raised, in February 1955, design work was too far advanced for things to be changed. Although no concerns were raised about the unique lining style used at the time, by 1959 vehicles were being repainted into the standard scheme as used on other classes which had two bodyside lines. At the same time Eastern Region units also gained 'speed whiskers'. This revised colour scheme is seen applied to Driving Trailer E79263, which was photographed at Stratford Shed on May 17 1958.

Opposite bottom: A classic view of the Metro-Cammell yellow diamond DMU, a class which for many years dominated the branch line scene in East Anglia. This set, seen in original form and with Driving Trailer leading, was captured at Dereham North while working a service to Norwich. Although closed in 1969 Dereham station had had a second lease of life as the headquarters of the Mid-Norfolk Railway, which opened in 1997. The signal box has also had an interesting second life. Following decommissioning it was sold and moved to Mattishall where it was used as a darkroom and study. It was then sold on in July 2006 for £11,000 and moved to Hindolveston, near Fakenham, where it is in use as an office.

Chapter Three
BR Built Low-Density Sets

Three distinct variations of DMU were produced, namely express, low-density and suburban. The largest number made were of the low-density type, with British Railways itself contributing thousands of vehicles from its Litchurch Lane works at Derby.

Above: Derby moved on to building its first all steel vehicles in 1956, which were also the first built by that works on the longer 63ft underframe. These were 49 low-density sets for the Eastern Region's Lincolnshire and South Humber services, which featured Leyland 150hp engines and what was to become the new 'standard' Derby cab arrangement. Due to a lack of power the final one was delivered with bigger Albion 230hp engines and subsequently the rest were upgraded to suit. The class can readily be identified in original form by the lack of front marker lights apart from the one above the cab. An example is seen at Mablethorpe Station in September 1958, during the period that two-car sets were running with an additional power car due to deficiencies in performance when fitted with the Leyland engines. A tail load of one van is also being hauled.

Opposite top: Speed whiskers appeared in the early 1960s as examples passed through the paint shop, at which time they received the coaching stock roundel instead of the previously carried locomotive type. These units, later to be known as the Class 114, were also the first to feature the two-character headcode box which was designed to enable railway staff to identify a particular service by the numbers and letters displayed. Here an example is seen leaving Retford on a working to Lincoln Central on August 25 1962. The 114s were to be very successful and remained on their intended workings, as well as services around Birmingham, until the last was withdrawn in 1992.

Opposite bottom: Later in their lives the 114s gained standard marker lights above the buffers, losing the one on the roof, the two-character headcode blinds were also removed and the centre cab panel was plated over. Examples of the class appeared in many different liveries including blue, blue and grey and South Yorkshire PTE. Some were also later converted into parcels cars by having roller shutter doors inserted in the sides and having strengthened floors. In this form they also appeared in Royal Mail red, one later going into departmental use where even more colour variations were worn, before finally passing into preservation. Driving Trailer E56040 is seen here on shed in Lincoln towards the end of its career.

Above: An updated version of the original 'Derby Lightweight' was put into production in 1958 which used the by-now standard Derby steel cab and which had an updated electrical system of the 'blue square' type. This was basically similar to the 'yellow diamond' but used relays on each individual car to draw power from the local battery to work components instead of relying on power being transmitted down the whole length of the train from the leading vehicle. The cab front contained a two-character headcode panel below the windows, as used on the 114, but this time marker lights were incorporated from new. The body was very similar to that of the first 'lightweights' apart from the cab and rear steel end, although the seats used were of a less elaborate design, being more akin to those fitted to buses. The first batch delivered was of 62 power-trailer sets, three pairs of which are seen here when brand new in 1958 leaving Southport Station. In the rear of the shot is Southport St Luke's signal box which was an electro-pneumatic box with 103 levers installed by Westinghouse Brake and the Saxby Signal Company in 1902.

Opposite bottom: The updated lightweight design soon became one of the most numerous ever to have been provided, with a total of 333 cars built over a two-year period. Early batches featured a destination blind housed in a fibre glass roof section above the cab, as well as the two-character headcode display. M50942 was a Driving Motor Brake which was part of an order for 50 power-trailer sets for the London Midland Region which came roughly halfway through the build programme. When new these DMUs were very popular for excursions due to their panoramic windows and this one was photographed at Harrow and Wealdstone while engaged on a trip to Eastbourne in August 1963. Harrow and Wealdstone was opened by the London and Birmingham Railway in July 1837 and is still open today as part of the West Coast Main Line. It was, of course, tragically the scene of Britain's worst peacetime rail accident when in October 1952 112 people were killed when three trains collided at the station.

Above: Class 108s built from 1960 onwards had a slightly modified front end, with the two-character headcode display removed and a four-character version incorporated as part of the glass fibre cab roof. This involved moving the destination blind into a special box that was incorporated at the top of the centre window. Here that destination has been set to one showing where this power-twin set was manufactured, rather than to where it was going, with the unit being seen passing Monsal Dale signal box on the former Midland line between Manchester and Derby when obviously brand new. This unit appears to be one of 29 power-twins supplied to the London Midland Region in 1960 which were built concurrently with a batch of 21 power-trailers intended for less challenging routes. The vehicle nearest the camera is a Driving Motor Brake built against lot number 30601.

Above: The later 108s soon lost their attractive white cab roofs, which proved almost impossible to keep clean, and also gained yellow warning panels in place of speed whiskers. Not a great deal of use was made of the four-character headcode system which was designed to allow signalmen to be able to identify trains as they went past, but which were soon rendered obsolete by the advent of remote power signalling, which removed the requirement for trains to be visually identified. On April 22 1966 a four-coach set, with a power-trailer leading, is arriving at Southport with the 6.10pm train from Manchester. Power-trailer sets carried the coaching stock roundel only on the sides of the power cars while power-twins had it on both vehicles.

Opposite top: A two-car Class 108 set from one of the earlier batches is seen while working the 9.35am Bradford Forster Square to Ilkley train at Burley Junction on May 20 1966 and passes permanent way wagons which were at that time being used for the removal of track from the closed Arthington line. This 108 has had a slightly larger yellow panel painted on than that in the previous picture to make up for the green retained round the two-character panel. The cab roof has also lost its white colour and, as was typical for the period, the whole train was presented to the public in a very run-down and dirty condition.

Opposite bottom: British Rail's new corporate image began to appear on Derby-built products in 1966, with the Class 108s exhibiting a surprising number of variations of the plain blue livery. Many of the early repaints had this unusual arrangement in which the double arrow symbol was on the cab doors instead of the bodysides, and which utilised three-inch letters instead of the later and standard four inch. Later repaints also saw the yellow warning panel extended to cover the whole front end. In this scheme trains looked particularly drab and their appearance did nothing to promote the modern image that BR was attempting to promote. On February 25 1967 a power-trailer set, with the power car leading, departs from Preston station.

Opposite top: In an attempt to shake off the dirty and unacceptable image that British Rail had, many DMUs were refurbished, with the scheme including better internal lighting, brighter wall coverings, retrimmed seats and a rather impractical all-over white livery featuring a thick blue stripe. The Class 108s were included in this upgrade, with the first being dealt with in 1975. By this time the redundant route indicator displays below the cab windows were being removed and the units had acquired all-over yellow front ends. The new colours quickly proved impractical and never looked clean, and so eventually the decision was taken to repaint the fleet in BR's blue and grey scheme, which originally had been intended only for express passenger stock. Here one of the first Class 108s built is seen leaving Burley in Wharfdale on May 21 1980. Leading is Driving Trailer 56210 and providing the power is Driving Motor Brake 50621.

Opposite bottom: The final colour scheme for the Class 108s was standard BR blue and grey, which suited the class well. Here a London Midland allocated power-trailer set calls at Carnforth station with a train from the Cumbrian coast bound for Preston. Leading is Driving Motor Brake M50957 which has had a crude modification to plate over the recess which formerly housed the two-character headcode box. Class 108s lasted in service until 1993 and many have passed into preservation due to the durability of their aluminium bodies and the lack of asbestos in their construction. The train is paused near to the station clock, made famous for its appearance in the wartime classic 'Brief Encounter' which was filmed at the station.

Above: Derby's last design of DMU for urban working was the Class 107, which was basically a steel-bodied version of the final version of the Class 108, although there were differences in the window height on the body and the layout of the guard's van and its windows. A total of 26 three-car sets were constructed for suburban services in the Glasgow area, and the type was to be associated with Scotland for the whole of its life. When new all worked from Hamilton depot but later they were spread around other Scottish depots. As with many other DMU classes the 107s became very popular for use in 'land cruises' and excursions, some of which reached unusual territory. On July 18 1961 two sets were employed on such a working from Glasgow to Perth and Comrie, a location that had once been very popular with Victorian travellers. The two sets are seen at Comrie waiting for their return journey.

In common with other classes of DMU the 107s were modified several times during their lives, including having their headcode boxes plated over and receiving various different liveries. The original BUT engines were replaced by Leyland 680s during their lives while some received a third type of engine, the Leyland 4041, towards the end of their careers. Mass withdrawal of the Class 107s began in January 1991 with the class replaced by newly-introduced Sprinters and continued until the end of 1992, at which point some were converted for Sandite use. This shot, taken at Crookston, to the South west of Glasgow, shows second-built Sc51987, then part of set 107427, speeding away from the camera in typically semi-urban surroundings.

Chapter Four

Contractor Built Low-Density Sets

British Railways itself lacked the capacity to build the huge numbers of low-density sets that were required under the Modernisation Plan. As a result, tenders were sought from private firms with some being awarded huge orders, in particular Metropolitan-Cammell, the Birmingham Railway Carriage and Wagon Company and Cravens of Sheffield.

Metropolitan-Cammell built a total of 760 vehicles which were an updated version of their original 'lightweight' design between 1956 and 1959. Changes included a revision to the electrical arrangements so that they corresponded with the new 'blue square' standard, a revision to the cab controls and the omission of the skirt below the buffer beam at each end. Initial batches were built with four marker lights at each end, and this arrangement was continued until May 1957, with more than 80 sets built to this pattern. Many of these were delivered with three or four coaches, although vehicles were mixed up indiscriminately as time went on. Here a three-car set, with an early Driving Motor Composite leading, approaches Levisham station on what is now the North Yorkshire Moors Railway with a working from Whitby to Malton.

Above: Following the decision to adopt the two-character headcode box further batches were built which did not have either a bottom centre or a top marker light but instead had the new headcode box below the centre cab window. The Scottish Region received a large number of vehicles to this design, with 30 power-trailers arriving in 1958 and 33 three-car sets the following year. All the Metro-Cams, as they became known, initially had plain green front ends and had the same lining style used on the original 'yellow diamond' cars when they were new. As might be expected there were a large number of minor variations during the build between class members, including to the guard's doors, vacuum pipes and layout of the guard's van. In original condition a four-car set leaves the bridge and passes Tay Bridge South Junction, which was the junction with the Newport line, a route which closed in 1969.

Opposite top: Due to the number of accidents to railway workers caused by the relatively silent approach of the new units, 'speed whiskers' were added fairly early in their careers, although many could be seen without for some years after the decision was taken to add them. Diesel Multiple Units proved to be very popular with the public and were something of a novelty when introduced to many regions. A 'Metro-Cam' set in pristine green livery was used to ferry passengers to an event held at Dawsholm Shed, which was on the former Glasgow Central Railway, in 1959 in connection with the Scottish Industries Exhibition. At that time the shed was home to a number of historic steam locomotives, which included Caledonian Railway 'single' 123 and a 'Jones Goods', which can also be seen in steam in the picture.

Opposite bottom: Whenever the new units were brought into service British Railways tried to obtain some publicity, usually by inviting a party of local dignitaries to partake in one of the first runs. Here two mayors and their civic party inspect a brand-new Metro-Cammell unit which is ready to work a service to Leeds City station. The North Eastern Region received a large number of these units which were set to work around the Leeds, Darlington and Newcastle areas and these formed the mainstay of these services until displaced by Pacers and Sprinters in the 1990s. Two, three and four-car versions were produced with many of the two-car sets being power-twins due to the heavily-graded lines found around the Pennines. The blue square coupling code is prominent, with this feature first appearing in January 1957.

Opposite top: One of Scotland's power-trailer sets is seen at Haymarket depot in 1962 when still in plain green livery and without any form of warning markings at the end. These Metro-Cammell vehicles would later become well known as Class 101s but originally, they were also allocated Class 102, which was a designation used for those units which had AEC engines fitted, rather than Leylands. This situation was regularised from the 1970s when the AEC-engined vehicles received Leyland power units during works visits, after that the Class 102 designation fell out of use. Haymarket was a former steam shed in Edinburgh that was redeveloped solely for use by diesels in 1963, it is still in use today as one of the main bases for Scotrail's DMU fleet.

Opposite bottom: In as-delivered condition Driving Trailer Sc56397 and its partner Driving Motor Brake Sc51239 were pictured at Aberdeen station while waiting to depart with a service to Ballater on July 19 1958. This set had replaced the remaining steam workings on the Deeside Line 12 days earlier and was at that time working turn-about with the battery-electric pictured in Chapter Two. The run to Ballater was 43 miles long and took in some exceptional scenery, but inevitably the line was slated for closure under the Beeching plans, with its final train running in 1967. Now a short part of it, centred round Banchory, has been re-opened as a heritage line, with hopes that it can be extended at some time in the future.

Above: Although the Western Region proper didn't receive an allocation of Metro-Cammells until 1975 the sets were deployed to work on former Great Western Lines which had passed through reorganisation in 1963 to the London Midland Region. One of the places served by these units was Oswestry, at one time a massive junction with its own locomotive works and an extensive number of services radiating from it. The Beeching cuts left only a shuttle from Gobowen which was usually worked by these units and final closure came in 1966 when the town's two passenger stations, along with the works, closed down. Today the heritage Cambrian Railway occupies the sole track which is left and fittingly has two Metro-Cammell units in its collection which it intends to use for services.

Opposite: In June 1957 the Eastern Region received a batch of ten power-twin sets which were based at Darlington Shed and which became much favoured for use on the hilly coast route between Whitby and Scarborough. Use of DMUs enabled much time-saving on these workings as a change of direction was required shortly after climbing from Whitby to the West Cliff station in order to reach Scarborough and, of course, units did not require a locomotive to run round the train for this to be achieved. By the time of this photograph yellow panels had begun to be applied to the cab ends and 'overhead electrification' flashes had also appeared. With Driving Motor Brake E50252 leading, one of these sets leaves Whitby station sometime in the early 1960s. Whitby is still open today and serves both Northern Rail's service from Middlesbrough and also the North Yorkshire Moors Heritage Service from Pickering.

Above: The branch line to the university town of St Andrew's in Scotland is interesting in that it was constructed by an independent company and thus was built to a very low budget, which later led to many problems with the infrastructure. Traffic levels were never very good and were severely hit by road competition in the 20th century. Metro-Cammell DMUs were introduced on June 15 1959 with the hope that they would cut costs and increase revenue, with shuttles from Leuchars being the regular form of working. One of these sets is seen working the 1220 service from Leuchars to St Andrews on June 1 1968. Six months later the passenger service was withdrawn. Goods traffic had ceased two years earlier, as evidenced by the lines which had already been lifted.

Above: Metro-Cammell units typified the 1960s railway scene, such as this example which is seen at Birkenhead Woodside station. This terminus served the former Great Western route to Chester and onwards to Wolverhampton and Paddington but by this time had been relegated to secondary status. It was opened on March 31 1878 but after March 1967 ceased to serve through traffic to London with only the DMU services to Chester and Helsby remaining. These ceased on November 5 1967 and the station was demolished within a couple of years. The Metro-Cammell units lasted a great deal longer with the last of them not being withdrawn until December 2003.

Opposite top: Along with the rest of the DMU fleet the Metro-Cammell units began to appear in Rail Blue livery from 1967 onwards. Early repaints had only a small yellow warning panel but most were finished in this style with the yellow area covering the whole cab end. The route indicator box stayed in place for a few years but all were eventually removed and plated over. Here Driving Motor Brake E50281 is seen at Dringhouses with a York to Selby service, a common duty for this type of unit. Although outwardly more or less identical to the Class 101 this is in fact a Class 111, being fitted with Rolls-Royce C6 engines of 180hp instead of the 150hp Leyland. It is one of a batch of 10 three-car sets which were delivered new to the North Eastern Region in 1958 and 1959.

Opposite bottom: In 1974 a three-car Class 101 was turned out in white livery with a blue stripe. It had a fully refurbished interior with improved seating and lighting and was intended to be the prototype for a mass upgrade of the fleet. In the event most of the upgrade plans were not adopted and instead individual vehicles were merely repainted. This new livery was short-lived as, not surprisingly, it proved difficult to keep clean. Pictured at York depot is Metro-Cammell Driving Trailer E56220 which dates from 1957, but which by this time had had front end modifications to remove the route indicator box, leaving a somewhat plain front end. Most two-car sets were made up of one powered and one unpowered vehicle, while three-car sets had a power car at both ends. In view of this this, body design, which also had a first-class compartment, was produced in either powered or unpowered versions.

Opposite top: The next livery style adopted was that of the much more attractive blue and grey, which was applied generally from 1978 onwards and which suited the Metro-Cammell units well. This shot of a Class 111 version is particularly interesting in that it shows one of the three-car sets which was reduced to two vehicles as an economy measure, in a scheme which commenced in 1982. Sets thus shortened had one of the two Rolls-Royce engines in each car removed and were renumbered in the 78XXX series. Here 78711 and 78961, formerly numbered 53275 and 53280, are seen at Ilkley station in West Yorkshire on November 17 1985. All these units were allocated to Neville Hill depot and were disposed of between 1986 and 1989.

Opposite bottom: As delivered the last batch of Class 111s had a four-character headcode box fitted above the cab windows, but this soon fell into disuse as that form of train reporting was abandoned. Like the route indicator before it, this fitting was removed and plated over as units visited the workshops for overhaul but these 111s could always be identified by the fact that the destination indicator was fitted lower down than on the 'standard' model. Here one of the 111s, already reduced to two-car formation, is seen passing Esholt while working a Bradford Forster Square to Ilkley train on February 18 1983. The final examples of this class lasted until 1995, being replaced by 'Pacers' and 'Sprinters'.

Above: Birmingham Railway Carriage and Wagon works was successful in obtaining an order for 302 DMU vehicles, and these later were better known as Class 104. Two, three and four-car versions were produced with sets being allocated to the North Eastern and the London Midland Regions, with all being delivered over a period of three years. Standard Leyland 150hp engines were used and the class proved to be very successful, although they had shorter lives than some others due to never being selected for refurbishment. They are perhaps best-known for their almost virtual monopoly of the Manchester-Buxton route, but in fact they worked far and wide over the system. Here Driving Motor Composite M50531, which is part of a three-car set, is pictured stabled at Nottingham Midland station when still in virtually as-built condition.

Opposite top: As delivered the Class 104 was in green livery, with the first few having the lion over wheel emblem, which was soon replaced with the familiar coaching roundel. Later vehicles had the speed whiskers from new and those which had been delivered without soon obtained them. The class was instantly recognisable by the upsweep in the lining at the front end. Driving Motor Brake Second M50479 was part of a three-car set delivered to the London Midland Region in 1957 and is seen here being operated in multiple with a similar class member, making up a six-car train. The driver seems to have some issues as he has called out a fitter, with both looking in the direction of the number two engine of this power car.

Opposite bottom: On September 28 1959 Driving Motor Brake M50447 is seen alongside 'Black Five' 44842 at Birmingham New Street Station in a scene which is totally unrecognisable today, as the station is now buried beneath a shopping complex. The station was first constructed in 1846 and was enlarged several times, reaching its largest by 1885 when it covered no less than 12 acres. Following removal of the overall roof in 1956 the site was subsequently reconstructed twice, in the mid-1960s and again in 2010-2015, leaving all platforms at basement level and underneath commercial development. Happily, the Class 104 vehicle survives, although currently as a non-runner, being preserved at the Llangollen Railway. It is seen here in original condition, having not yet had the speed whiskers added to its green livery.

Above: Diesel Multiple Units were regarded as ultra-modern when they first were introduced, although interest in them amongst enthusiasts soon waned, as steam locomotives began to be phased out. In what looks to be a specially-staged publicity photograph, a group of eager schoolboys chat with the driver of a Class 104, prior, it would seem, to some sort of sporting trip. In their later days the Class 104s were allocated far and wide with allocations being made as far North as Ayr and as far South as Old Oak Common near London. Some were specially modified for commuter services between Blackpool and Manchester by having improved suspension while some others, like the Class 111s, had their formations reduced to two cars and had one engine removed from each power car.

Opposite top: From 1966 onwards Class 104s were given the plain blue livery, at first with a small yellow warning panel but very soon afterwards with a full yellow end. Of interest is that vehicles intended for different regions had different interior finishes, the ones for the London Midland Region used a veneer finish while those for the North Eastern had the more standard Formica. Withdrawals started with Newcastle-allocated vehicles which had been made surplus by the construction of the Tyne and Wear Metro in 1980 and continued steadily until the final versions were taken out of service by Network Southeast ten years later. Here two sets are seen on their traditional stamping ground at Wigan Wallgate station in May 1975, with the station looking much more unkept than it does in modern times.

Opposite bottom: BRCW produced an updated and modernised version of the Class 104 which was designated Class 110. These were built for use on the former Lancashire and Yorkshire Trans-Pennine routes, and gained the nickname of the 'Calder Valley' sets. The major differences to the earlier units were the use of alloy window frames, a revised cab and the substitution of Rolls-Royce power equipment, which was required to give additional horsepower for the hilly terrain in which the units were expected to operate. Thirty sets were constructed with 20 going to the North Eastern Region and the remainder to the London Midland. These sets were amongst the last conventional DMUs constructed, making an appearance in 1961 and 1962. A brand-new Class 110 is pictured on trial near Derby on July 24 1961.

Above: The Class 110s entered service on January 1 1962 and mainly worked services from York, Leeds and Bradford via the Calder Valley to Manchester and Liverpool. Some routes also took them out as far as Blackpool. A clock-face hourly timetable was introduced, along with journey time reductions, leading to a large increase in passenger numbers. A novel feature was the provision of two first-class saloons, one at each end, with one intended for smokers and the other for those who did not. These DMUs are considered by many to be amongst the most stylish ever to have been built. On August 25 1962 a single three-car set with Driving Motor Brake E51815 leading is seen just south of York.

Above: The Class 110s remained intact until 1963 when one set was involved in a fire. However, the first power car to be taken out of service in the normal course of events was Driving Motor Composite E51848 which was withdrawn in 1972 due to its condition and the fact that there was a surplus of this type of car at that time. The class continued on in passenger service for many years after that, although with many sets reduced to only two coaches, with the last one not being disposed of until 1990, with four vehicles then enjoying a brief second career within Sandite units. In happier times on September 6 1964 the first coach withdrawn, E51848, is seen within Bradford City Goods Yard heading an RCTS tour of the West Riding, which obviously covered some unusual tracks!

Opposite top: Another manufacturer to benefit from a large order for diesel multiple units was Cravens of Sheffield, which was already heavily involved in work for British Railways. The firm contributed 405 vehicles in total of which 302 would be later designated as the Class 105 with this class working in many areas including East Anglia, East Yorkshire, the London suburbs and Scotland. In time examples were allocated to many other areas, particularly following the Beeching closures. The first batch of these units was shared between the Eastern and the London Midland regions with those allocated to the Eastern being turned out with four marker lights and no speed whiskers or yellow warning panel. In original condition one of the first batch is seen receiving the single line token while working a service to Withernsea, shortly after introduction which took place on January 7 1957.

Opposite bottom: Cravens units for the London Midland Region were fitted with a two-character headcode box below the cab windows, and this style was adopted for all subsequent builds, although there were detail differences between batches. On June 8 1958 two pairs, 50771/50804 and 50773/50806, were employed to work the RCTS 'Roses Railtour' which started at Manchester Victoria and covered over 200 miles of line in the North of England, including many branches, freight facilities and loco sheds, and which is seen here while enjoying a layover at Harrogate station. At the time of this photograph the units would have been only a few months old as the first of this batch was only delivered in September 1957.

Above: As built some members of the class had AEC and some Leyland engines, although the majority had AEC equipment and the exhaust pipes were unusually led through the guard's compartment and terminated at roof level, rather than being at the rear of the power car. Many of the sets were allocated to East Anglia and set to work on lines which would soon close under the Beeching Axe, and here a brand-new set is seen at Maldon East and Heybridge Station undergoing careful scrutiny by a member of the station staff. This station was at the end of a branch from Witham and became better known for its use of four-wheel railbuses in its final years. Opening in 1848 it was somewhat palatial, due it is said to the vice-chairman of the railway seeking support for his campaign to become the local MP, but along with many other lines in the area it suffered badly from competition from the roads in the early part of the 20th century. DMUs arrived in 1957 with the railbuses the year after but could not save the line, which closed in 1964.

Opposite top: Cravens products became well-known by enthusiasts for their propensity to rattle, particularly from the windows, and for the vibration from the engines. The type shared the body profile and many of the components of the company's Mark One coaches with delivery commencing in August 1956 and with production being continuous until June 1959 by which time 108 power trailer, 14 power twins, 19 three-car sets and a spare Driving Motor Brake had been constructed. By 1960, when this two-car set was photographed leaving Cambridge with a train for Ipswich, the type had become synonymous with local services in East Anglia, with many having been fitted with a special panel just behind the cab door, to cushion the effects of tokens impacting the sides of vehicles during exchanges on the move.

Opposite bottom: The London Midland Region deployed some of its Cravens units on longer-distance work, with this pair of power-trailer sets being used on September 21 1960 for a service from Liverpool Lime Street to Birmingham on a route which today sees electric trains. Leaving Lime Street Station, the unit appears to have a tail lamp still in position, although there is a driver at the controls, so perhaps it was being re-platformed prior to departure. Standing at an adjacent platform is a filthy Stanier 'Black Five' which is working a Class 1 express. Both trains would face a climb of over a mile on a gradient of 1:88, during which the performance of the DMU would far exceed that of the steam engine, and which was one of the reasons that journey times could be cut when the diesels were introduced.

Above: Many of the final batch of the Cravens Class 105s were delivered to Scottish sheds, first making an appearance in June 1959 and being used on lines between Aberdeen and Peterhead and also on some branch lines such as the Ballater branch, where one set worked alongside the battery-electric described earlier. Some were also used around the Glasgow suburban network. During 1959 one regular turn for the Cravens was the 'Six Lochs Tour' which saw a service from Glasgow to Crianlarich run for sightseers every Sunday. Usually this was made up of four power-twins and was well-loaded. Here one such working is seen at Cove, a small village on Loch Long which was once home to many of the wealthy merchants from Glasgow, who commuted into the city by train each day.

Above: In the late 1950s the cull of branch lines and other services in the East of the country had already started which led to a number of the Cravens units being surplus to requirements, despite the fact that they were only by this time less than three years old. A total of 28 units were redeployed to work suburban services from King's Cross, for which work they were coupled in multiple and proved eminently unsuitable, with the transfer being completed by early 1959. This arrangement lasted until electrification in 1977 at which point the sets moved on to various depots including Lincoln, Ayr and Tyseley. Although Hornsea Town, the terminus of a branch from Hull, survived the first round of closures, it eventually succumbed to the Beeching Axe in October 1964. A power-trailer set from the first batch of Class 105s built is seen here leaving the station only a year before it closed forever. The station building was listed and still survives, being fully restored in the late 1980s.

Opposite top: In common with many other classes of DMU the Class 105s began to receive Rail blue livery from 1966 onwards. At first London Midland vehicles had a small yellow panel but Eastern Region ones painted at Doncaster had a much bigger yellow section, which covered the whole front and below the windscreens. Eventually a full yellow end became the normal, although here Driving Motor Brake E53363, seems to have acquired a white cab roof. The Cravens units were never selected for refurbishment and as a consequence never received blue and grey livery. Withdrawals started in the early-1980s and the whole class was gone within eight years, principally because of the requirement to rid the railway network of vehicles which had been insulated with blue asbestos.

Above: Cravens also received an order for 50 power twins to a revised design, with half of these being intended for Liverpool-St Helen's services, and the rest for the LMR's central division, with these being shedded at Newton Heath and Accrington. These differed from the earlier design in that they were fitted with only one engine per power car, with that being a 238hp Rolls-Royce type, and with both cars being powered. The first 25 sets had mechanical transmission and looked very similar to the earlier sets but the final 25 were fitted with hydraulic transmission and could easily be identified by the large headcode box that was fitted above the cab windows and which incorporated both route and destination indications. In the hilly terrain for which these sets were ordered overheating was frequent, and the Rolls-Royce hydraulic transmission was a constant source of difficulty. In as-delivered condition one of the hydraulic sets, later Class 113, makes a photographic stop while working a special.

Above: Accrington shed played host to all these units in their early days and here Driving Motor Composite M51778 rests alongside other examples of the type. Between 1962 and 1967, 17 of the 25 hydraulic sets were transferred to Cricklewood in London, a depot which also had the Rolls-Royce engined/hydraulic Class 127s but they were soon exchanged for all the mechanical sets and then in 1968 sent back home again or taken out of service where they were. The class became known for poor availability and suffered a number of propeller shaft failures, one of which resulted in a serious fire, due to the design routing the shaft through a tunnel made in the fuel tank.

Chapter Five

Contractor Built Low-Density Vehicles, smaller batches

While some manufacturers received orders for a large number of vehicles, others were responsible for only a handful of those constructed. Some, such as D. Wickham and Co, were unable to manufacture to the required timescale while others, such as the Gloucester Railway Carriage and Wagon Company, provided designs that were not totally satisfactory.

Above: The Gloucester Railway Carriage and Wagon Company received an order for 20 two-car power-trailer sets during June 1956, which were later to be designated as Class 100. These were to an innovative design in which tubular body sections were used to provide structural strength, thus doing away with a conventional underframe and saving weight. This produced a two-car set which weighed only 55 tons when fully completed, giving a fairly high power to weight ratio compared with other types. The AEC 150hp engines were used, with the rest of the mechanicals being compatible with other types then in build. A further 20 sets were ordered in January 1957, even before the first ones had been delivered, and these immediately followed on from the first on the factory production line. On June 20 1959 one of these sets is seen in original condition while working a Corstorphine to Edinburgh service as it passes Princes Street gardens in Edinburgh.

Opposite bottom: Given the appalling reliability record of these Rolls-Royce engine units it was not surprising that they were slated for early withdrawal. Of those mechanical units allocated to Cricklewood most were withdrawn in November 1968 when they were not even ten years old and the rest were gone within a year. Accrington shed got rid of its hydraulics in 1969 when it was allocated a number of 'standard' Cravens power-twins in their place and the whole class was swiftly dispatched to the scrap yard and broken up. In 1960 the 113s, as the hydraulic sets would have become, were still seeing widespread use on the lines radiating from their Lancashire base, with examples being used as far out as on routes to Skipton, where Driving Motor Brake M51751 was seen, probably with Driving Motor Composite M51776 in tow, as cars were not frequently mixed up between sets with these classes.

Above: The first 20 sets can easily be identified by the provision of only one marker light on the cab ends, and that being above cab height, with unusually no markers being provided above the buffers. These units were originally intended to be allocated to Manchester but during the time they were in build the decision was taken to send 11 of them to Scotland, although these did spend a short amount of time in the North west until the Park Royal units were delivered. Here one of this early series is seen at Scotstoun East while working the 12:05 Yoker Ferry to Coatbridge Central suburban service on October 3 1964. As delivered the units had plain green front ends and were painted in a lighter shade of green than many other classes but yellow panels began to be added from the early 1960s, with many receiving the more common darker DMU green at the same time.

Opposite top: Second batch units had a more conventional illumination arrangement with two marker lights being provided above the buffers and with the high-level lamp being omitted. All these units were sent to Edinburgh where they were intensively used on suburban services. It seems that the driver of this example is going to have a tough time if it begins to rain for the driver's side windscreen wiper appears to have dropped off with the whole of the arm as well as the blade being missing! Despite this the unit duly worked the Leith North to Edinburgh Princes Street service on July 15 1958 as intended. Princes Street station opened in 1848 but was closed in 1965 when traffic was centralised on Waverley station. By this time much of the suburban network had also been dismantled.

Opposite bottom: Working through Morningside Road station, in the Edinburgh suburbs, this Gloucester 100 unit typifies the type of duty on which these vehicles were deployed. As well as short-distance work these units were also used in multiple on Glasgow to Edinburgh semi-fast services but were removed after complaints of rough riding. The London Midland-allocated units were based in the Manchester and Birmingham areas but some could also be found in North Wales. Generally, they worked local services but seemed to be unpopular and were constantly being moved on as other sets became available. Generally speaking these units suffered from poor build quality and within a short space of time corrosion issues began to come to the fore, not helped by the method used to secure the windows which allowed water to get into the bodywork.

Above: Working an Edinburgh-Glasgow service this pair of Gloucester 100 units is passing one of William Pickersgill's '72' Class 4-4-0s, which despite its antique appearance was only around 35 years old at this point. 54505 was one of 32 of its class constructed between 1920 and 1922 while the DMU is from the second batch of Class 100s built, and is still to acquire any form of front-end warning stripes or panel. These units featured very large cab front windows but side vision in the front compartments was severely compromised by the need to provide additional strength above the jacking points on the solebar below, which resulted in one of the windows being much smaller than the others.

Opposite top: Instantly recognisable by the rounded shape of the lower body, the Gloucester Class 100s were launched into service with much fanfare, particularly in Scotland where one was exhibited at Edinburgh Waverley station prior to the class being introduced into service. Scotland soon became the home of the class as many of the London Midland-allocated sets were sent there to join their sisters but the 1960s electrification of the Glasgow area rendered some of them surplus with the result that many class members were transferred to Newcastle and then to Cambridge, where many were to see out their days. Second batch Driving Motor Brake Sc51109 rests between duties at an unknown location with Edinburgh Waverley on the destination blind.

Opposite bottom: Driving Trailer 56303 left Scotland for Newcastle in July 1967, moving on to Cambridge in October 1970 and is seen at Lowestoft in November 1978. Withdrawal of those sets that remained in Scotland began in earnest in 1972 when eight were taken out of service. Various reinstatements took place until the survivors were finally sent off to Leeds, Norwich and Tyseley but service there didn't last for long. None were selected for refurbishment, but two sets were preserved from 1975 onwards, initially at the North Yorkshire Moors Railway, but today only one survives, and is being painfully restored from scrap condition, with a particular issue being corrosion, just as it was for British Railways in their service days.

Above: Another manufacturer trying an integral steel body design was Park Royal Motors, which was awarded an order for 20 power-trailer sets, which were new to the Birmingham area but which were later to become synonymous with services in North Wales and Cheshire, although some were used on the St Albans and Watford branches. One of these, headed by Driving Trailer Composite M56166, is pictured at Belmont while working a train on August 11 1958. This class was later to be designated as Class 103 although they were very short-lived, suffering like the Gloucesters from excessive corrosion. They can easily be identified by the pronounced droop in the lining above the cab windows. Although some sets were delivered without 'speed whiskers' the rest of them had them from new, with the remainder receiving them later.

Opposite top: The other end of the same set is seen again at Belmont and with Driving Motor Brake M50411 leading, demonstrating how run down these sets had become in service. Bogie fractures added to the woes suffered by these units, and as a result no further orders were received by Park Royal, with their only other contribution to the modernisation plan units being a small number of four-wheel railbuses. By January 1966 all the Park Royals had been reallocated together to Chester depot but in 1970 four sets went to the Western Region, being used around Reading. Belmont was on the former LNWR branch to Stanmore and traffic through there was already so light that one platform was out of use at the time this picture was taken.

Lower: This unusual shot shows a Park Royal, by now with a yellow warning panel, leaving Oxford with a Cambridge-bound service, which would have been unusual work for this class. Like the Gloucesters before them the Park Royals were not selected for refurbishment or retention and suffered early withdrawal. Two sets passed into departmental use as early as 1971 while withdrawals started the following year, although it was 1983 before the last of them was taken out of regular passenger service. Two sets passed to the West Somerset Railway for preservation in 1975 although advanced rust caused one of them to be scrapped in 1993, while the other hung on long enough for some restoration work to be done on it, following which it went to the Helston Railway as a static exhibit. A third set was saved from departmental service in 1986, although this was heavily pillaged and the power car was subsequently scrapped. One trailer is privately preserved in North Wales.

Opposite top: Wickham of Ware are best known for their range of track inspection trolleys, but they also have a history of supplying railcars, particularly for service overseas, using their novel method of aluminium lightweight construction. British Railways ordered five sets from this manufacturer in 1957, all of which initially went to the Eastern Region. They were not particularly successful and two were quickly bought back by the manufacturers for re-sale to Trinidad and Tobago. When first built the sets were easily identifiable by their polished aluminium window surrounds, and it is in this condition that one is seen at Emerson Park station while on an Upminster to Romford working in early 1958. This station is more or less unchanged today, apart from featuring electrification masts, and is now part of the London Overground system, with two trains an hour each way being provided. At the time the Wickham was pictured less than 30,000 people a year used the station, today the figure is ten times that.

Opposite bottom: The appearance of the Wickham units wasn't helped by the application of corporate blue livery in the late 1960s. By this time there were only three Wickham sets left in service and one of them is seen calling at Middle Drove Station, which served the village of Tilney Fen End near Downham Market in Norfolk. Opened in 1848 the station inevitably was one of those which closed in 1968 under the Beeching axe, and it typifies the country stations in the East of the country which were so familiar to first-generation DMUs. One of the unusual features of the Wickham units was that the gutters over the cab front dipped down below the destination boxes, a feature that made them almost useless for their intended purpose of keeping rain off the front windows. This unidentified example is heading for King's Lynn and is seen passing a Cravens unit which is working a service for March.

Above: One of the regular duties for the Wickhams was that between Braintree and Bishops Stortford but with the sets being allocated to Cambridge they could be found operating turn about with other types on services all over the East. In May 1970 only two were left in passenger service and these were transferred to Norwich for their final year. Wickhams worked their final passenger trains in October 1971 and so are not as well known as many other types. These cars were extremely light but due to their box-section construction and hand-finished interiors would have been very difficult to maintain. Because they were such a small fleet, and non-standard apart from mechanical components, they were earmarked for early withdrawal.

Top: In 1967 one of the three surviving Wickham sets was taken to Doncaster works where it was extensively overhauled and converted into a saloon for the use of the Eastern Region General Manager. The conversion involved the removal of the interior and the installation of a kitchen, lounge, dining table and bar, while the exterior was modified by having some of the doors plated over and others changed position. Not surprisingly the troublesome front gutters were modified at the same time. Driving Motor Brake E50416 became 975005 in the departmental series whilst its trailer E56171 became 975006 and the set was to enjoy a further 13 years use in this form, thus outliving the two surviving passenger sets by some ten years.

Bottom: As a saloon the Wickham set travelled all over the Eastern Region, being used for charters as well as for official inspections, but following some minor damage being sustained it was sidelined in 1980, shortly afterwards being purchased by the Chasewater Railway. Thirteen years later and in much the same condition as before, it was bought by Llangollen Railcars, a charity specialising in DMU restoration, being moved to the Midland Railway Centre for restoration, a process which cost almost £200,000, and which was supported by the National Lottery. Now fully restored to as built condition and with a replica interior to the original specification, this set is fully operable at the Llangollen Railway.

Chapter Six
Cross-Country Sets

The low-density style of DMU set was not considered suitable for all types of duty and as a consequence several designs were produced which were suitable for longer-distance journeys. Many of these gave standards of comfort which were comparable to locomotive-hauled coaches, and some even included compartments and buffet areas.

Swindon Works was tasked with the design and production of the first true cross-country or inter-city DMU, and this was to make its appearance in 1956 in the form of a six car set which had the unusual feature (for the time) of intermediate cabs being fitted which enabled the set to be split into two three-cars for part of the journey. Unlike other types of DMU there was no forward view through the driver's cab at one end due to the guard's van being placed immediately behind the driver. Numbered in the early 79XXX series these sets became synonymous with Glasgow to Edinburgh services, covering these duties exclusively for a period of 14 years until replaced by locomotives and stock. Despite this the first six sets did spend their first three years working services between Birmingham and South Wales, but were later transferred to join their classmates North of the border. Driving Motor Brake Sc79109 prepares to leave Glasgow Queen Street station when less than a year old. Of note is the total lack of train indicator lights with the only illumination to the front being by way of a lit route stencil.

The arrival of the Swindon Edinburgh-Glasgow sets must have been a culture shock to the enginemen of the period, one of whom is seen ready to commence duties with Driving Motor Brake Sc79098 at Glasgow Queen Street in the early days of operation. Power cars had an open arrangement with seating in 2+2 configuration with only one saloon, while the intermediate trailers had either seven first class compartments or a buffet section with three compartments, each train having one of each type of centre car. Corridor connections were provided on the intermediate driving cars enabling passengers to move from one part of the set to another when in full six-car formation, an arrangement that was to be later repeated on many of the second-generation classes of unit.

Opposite top: Delivered in the lighter version of BR green the 'Edinburgh-Glasgow' soon received the more familiar darker green livery and they went from that directly into BR blue and grey, being considered to be express passenger stock. A few vehicles which in later life became used within sets of other classes did, however, receive all-over blue. In 1971 work to replace them with Class 27 hauled push-pull sets commenced and consideration was then given to redeploying some sets on Far-North services, as a result of this a trial was organised which saw a set undergoing a trip to Thurso and Wick. However nothing came of this proposal and instead all were withdrawn. The trial set, in blue and grey livery, is pictured at Wick station headed by Driving Motor Brake Sc79097.

Opposite bottom: Although this picture shows a vehicle of one of the follow-up orders for similar units, which became Class 126, it shows clearly the arrangement adopted for the intermediate driving cabs, with crew positions provided each side of the central corridor connection. The Edinburgh-Glasgow units had only a single stencil position at each side whereas the later ones had proper four-character headcode panels provided. Although the intention always was that the sets would be marshalled the right way round so that the intermediate cabs would come together when sets were made up to full length this wasn't always possible, as is seen here at Barrhill where a six-car set is working with an intermediate cab leading. As more sets to this pattern were added their sphere of operation was extended to include other routes, including this one which is on the Ayr to Stranraer section of the Glasgow and South Western line.

Cross-Country Sets

An updated version of the Edinburgh-Glasgow sets appeared in 1959, with the major visual difference being that the guard's van was relocated to the rear of the Driving Motor Brake, enabling the popular 'front forward' view to be reinstated. A four-character headcode box was provided instead of the stencils and there was an additional access door for passengers in the centre of the power cars. These sets had some second-class compartments in the centre trailers instead of being all first class as had the earlier versions and all featured Pullman gangways and buckeye couplers as on the original units. Before being introduced to service some sets were stored briefly with both types of cab-end being visible in this shot which was taken at Lugton Goods Yard on May 30 1959. To the right is Driving Motor Brake Sc51031 while to the left is an intermediate-style cab on a Driving Motor Second. This type was later to become Class 126.

Cross-Country Sets

Top: Although yellow panels began to appear in the early 1960s there was no attempt to update the lighting on the coach ends, and the 126s ran with no marker lights or headlights until withdrawal. On August 21 1963 a Class 126 set, by now carrying the darker shade of DMU green, passes Pinwherry station, South Ayrshire. This station was opened by the Girvan and Portpatrick Junction Railway in October 1887 but wasn't very successful, closing and reopening no less than twice over the next 10 years. It finally closed to passenger traffic in September 1965 although its signal box lasted for another 27 years after that.

Bottom: Beginning in 1958 three batches of DMUs appeared, which were very similar in appearance to the Class 126s. Built again by Swindon works, the Class 120s were intended for cross-country work and were formed in three-car sets with a full width cab driving vehicle at each end. Fifty-eight of these were for the Western Region with the remaining seven allocated to the Scottish Region. Typical duties included semi-fast trains between Birmingham and South Wales, with some services terminating at Cardiff and others continuing on to Carmarthen and also use on the Central Wales line. The Scottish sets were put to work on the Aberdeen to Inverness route. Their comfortable interiors, which gave a level of comfort equal to locomotive-hauled trains of the time, made them popular for excursions such as this SLS special which is pictured at Blaenavon High Level on September 26 1964. By this time a full set of marker lights had been specified.

Above: All three coaches in each set were laid out in open style and there were no compartments. The first two batches contained a buffet car while the final ones built had full passenger accommodation in the middle coach. All were constructed with AEC engines but later had Leylands fitted in common with many other classes. Within a short space of time 22 sets were transferred to Derby, with the class becoming synonymous with Etches Park depot, and later there were moves for some to Chester and to the Manchester area. There were also some visual differences between batches with the final series having a four-character headcode box added to the front-end design. Here 1959-built Scottish-allocated Driving Motor Brake Sc51785 is seen working an Elgin-bound service and leaving Aberdeen on the route for which the Scottish examples had been built.

Opposite top: In common with many other DMUs the Class 120s became very run down under British Rail, although they did receive blue and grey livery rather than plain blue. Some vehicles did receive a refurbishment and asbestos removal but this was found to be not cost-effective and so the class was slated for withdrawal once replacement traction became available, with the majority being displaced by Sprinters in 1985 and 1986. Some displaced sets found themselves in Scotland where they had originally been sent for spares recovery, but which were then hurriedly reinstated for a short period of passenger service. One of these was Driving Motor Brake 53708, originally a Western Region vehicle and later allocated to the London Midland, which is seen here leaving Edinburgh Waverley, most likely during the latter half of 1986 when it was allocated to Haymarket depot. It was withdrawn in August the following year, with the rest of the class bar one preserved example being out of service by the end of 1989.

Opposite bottom: Due to a lack of capacity at Swindon works the Gloucester Railway Carriage and Wagon Company was contracted to build a series of cross-country units to the same general design as the Class 120, but these were built with the standard design of Derby cab front instead of that used by Swindon on the Class 120 and 126. A total of 28 sets were built though for some reason there were only 25 centre trailers, all of which were fitted with buffet facilities. All were allocated to the Western Region, with the first appearing in 1958, and they became common on several routes, including Bristol to Weymouth and the West Country as well as Cardiff to Pembroke Dock and the Cambrian Coast line. Like the 120s these units were very popular for special and excursion work which often took them far away from their usual routes. One such duty had brought this set, headed by Driving Motor Second W51104, to former Great Central territory where it is seen at Woodford Halse station, near Daventry, attracting the attention of a young enthusiast.

Opposite top: In common with other cross-country sets the Class 119s went straight from green livery to blue and grey, with the first re-liveried unit being seen in 1967. Over a period of time they lost their two-character headcode box, giving them a fairly plain appearance. Some sets were converted for use on Gatwick airport services by having the buffet counters removed in order to provide additional luggage storage space, while others worked as two-car sets. The class was not selected for refurbishment and so withdrawals began in the mid-1980s with the last of the class lasting only until 1995. Class 119s could often be seen on the Western main line and were very common in Reading where Driving Motor Second 51095 is pictured. Of interest is that this example has oval buffers, although all the class was built with round ones and most of them carried that type until withdrawal.

Opposite bottom: British Railways always envisaged the use of high-quality DMUs for cross-country and inter-city routes but early examples of the type from Swindon were lacking in external style, particularly at the front end. Designer E.G. Wilkes had been employed by BR to improve the appearance of traction units and had had a great deal of influence on many diesel classes, such as the Class 47. His input into Swindon's latest class of cross-country unit, the Class 124 for the Trans-Pennine route, resulted in this striking design with futuristic cab and wrap-round windows. A total of 17 six-car sets were built which were unusual in that the third and fourth vehicles were motorised, yet did not have a driving cab, and all were used on services between Hull and Liverpool.

Above: The spacious cab of the Class 124s was laid out in similar fashion to other units except that the instruments and controls were grouped in a much more ergonomic fashion and featured instrument housings similar to those which might have been seen on a contemporary car or motor coach. A particularly popular feature were the large windows between the passenger saloon and the cab which enabled customers to get an uninterrupted view of the track ahead. The introduction of the Trans-Pennine units enabled the number of services on the route to be increased and at the same time cut the time taken from coast to coast by 45 minutes. Almost 300 passengers could be accommodated in luxury and each set was equipped with a stylish buffet car.

Above: The Class 124s were responsible for a doubling of passenger numbers on the Trans-Pennine route with passengers praising the quality and speed of the ride but the building of the M62 motorway provided serious competition for the railways as car driving times from one side of the Pennines to the other were drastically reduced. As passenger numbers began to fall again British Railways looked at ways to save money and as a consequence the buffet cars were taken out of service and the sets shortened, this also allowed some of the intermediate power cars to be converted to trailers. Although normally confined to Hull-Liverpool duties these sets did much excursion work and have been noted at places such as Llangollen and the Conwy Valley branch in Wales, Ravenglass in Cumberland and as far North as Carlisle. In more normal territory, a set in original condition negotiates the arches to the North of Leeds station with a train bound for Hull.

Opposite top: In later years the Class 124s were combined with the Western Region's Class 123s to form a common pool and once displaced by locomotive-hauled sets on their original duties they were cascaded onto secondary routes such as the Hope Valley line and Leeds-Lancaster. All received blue and grey livery although mixed-livery sets were common, such as this seen at Selby on June 15 1967. As the class was heavily-contaminated with blue asbestos the cost of refurbishment was thought to be prohibitive and because of this none of them were ever given life-extension. By the 1980s each car had approximately 1.5m miles to its credit and the decision was taken to turn over their remaining duties to locomotives and stock with the result that all were withdrawn during 1980. Unfortunately a proposal to preserve one at the North Yorkshire Moors Railway came to nothing with the result that none of this class survived.

Opposite bottom: Swindon works built the final batch of first-generation DMUs for British Railways in 1963 which were also to an 'inter-city' design. The Class 123s comprised ten four-car sets, five of which contained a buffet car and five of which did not. Unlike the Trans-Pennine sets they were equipped with gangways at the driving ends, enabling passengers to walk through the complete train when sets were working in multiple. These units were put to work on services between Wales, Birmingham and Crewe as well as between Cardiff and Bristol, later moving to other duties in the Western Region. In 1977 they were transferred to Hull where they worked in a common pool with the Trans-Pennine sets, often being mixed with them. All were taken out of service by 1984. With Driving Motor Second W52104 leading, a Class 123 is seen running through the middle roads at Swindon station on June 12 1963.

Chapter Seven
Suburban Sets

For suburban work British Railways commissioned a series of DMUs, all based round a common design which originated at Derby works. Construction was carried out by British Railways itself, but also because of the number of vehicles required, by Pressed Steel and also the Birmingham Railway Carriage and Wagon works.

Suburban units were designed to have as many doors on each side of each vehicle as possible so as to aid rapid loading and unloading, and were originally intended for short-distance commuter work, although later many were allocated to other tasks.

Above: The replacement of steam by diesel units in certain suburban areas was announced in 1955, commencing with the Western Region. For this programme Derby works designed a three-car set, with power cars at each end and a trailer in the middle. Structurally and mechanically it was based on the earlier Class114, but with an amended body design to accommodate the suburban layout. Three batches of what was to become Class 116 were built totalling 320 vehicles, being powered by either AEC or Leyland 150hp engines and incorporating standard mechanical transmission. Livery as built was plain green as can be seen in this shot taken at Cardiff Queen Street of a number of units being washed. Driving Motor Brake Seconds W50854 and W50838 are in the foreground.

Opposite: Because British Railways' own workshops could not cope with the demand for suburban units several independent contractors were invited to tender for the construction of some of those required. The Pressed Steel Company of Linwood, near Paisley in Scotland, was successful in gaining a large order and built 123 vehicles in total of what was to become Class 117. These were prepared to drawings provided by Derby works but differed in that they were fitted with a four-character headcode box above the cab windows and initially no front marker lights. The Birmingham Railway Carriage and Wagon works added another 45 vehicles to the same design, which were designated Class 118. Here one of the Pressed Steel sets, led by Driving Motor Brake W51348, has arrived at Paddington. Delivered originally in lined green, these sets gained yellow panels from 1964 onwards.

Above: Although using the by-now standard suburban body layout the batch of what were to become Class 125 turned out by Derby works in 1958 mechanically differed significantly from previously-built classes. These 20 three-car sets were fitted with Rolls-Royce 238hp engines and hydraulic transmission with the intention that their performance would match the electric units with which they shared tracks for parts of their diagrams. They also used a unique control system which was largely pneumatic rather than being electrical. On these sets no first-class accommodation was provided, the centre trailer being entirely second class. The 125s spent their entire working lives on the GE Lea Valley lines and were scrapped by 1977. Driving Motor Second E50988 trails a six-car consist having arrived at London's Broad Street station on a service from Gordon Hill on April 29 1976.

Opposite top: Derby works also produced a number of four-car sets, including 41 which were to become known as Class 115. These had two centre trailers, one containing second class only and the other with some first-class accommodation. Because of the extra weight of the fourth car larger engines, in the form of Albion 230hp examples, were fitted to the power cars and the sets were fitted with standard four-speed Wilson mechanical gearboxes. The seats fitted to these sets were of a higher-backed variety than previous suburban sets and were therefore much more comfortable. The Class 115s were introduced in 1960 and were thus amongst the last diesel multiple units built. An interesting feature is that a Driving Motor Brake was provided at both ends, and it is one of these that is leading a set as it passes Beaconsfield with a Marylebone to High Wycombe working on April 26 1962.

Opposite bottom: Thirty four-car sets with a similar body layout to the Class 115s were also provided for the London St Pancras to Bedford suburban diesel scheme. These were provided with Rolls-Royce 238hp engines and hydraulic transmission in an attempt to provide increased acceleration from station stops and became Class 127. Based at Cricklewood they never strayed far from their intended route and remained there until displaced by electric units in the mid-1980s. The underfloor arrangement was never very satisfactory and fires and overheating were common. However, some units did survive long enough to become parcels units in the North west for a short time after withdrawal from passenger service. Here a Class 127 led by Driving Motor Brake M51623 passes Cricklewood Station with a train for St Pancras on February 4 1961.

Suburban units first made an appearance in the West Midlands and in South Wales as part of the Western Region Dieselisation Scheme. In the Birmingham area many services were introduced from Snow Hill station from Monday June 17 1957 on routes to Kidderminster, Bewdley and Dudley, with other routes being added as more sets became available. Although the Class 116s were the latest in modern technology their austere livery coupled with the rather run-down state of the railway system did little to promote their attractions. An issue which soon became significant was the lack of corridor connections between coaches, and the partitions between sections of coaches, which prevented movement from one part of the train to another. All the Class 116s were delivered in plain green but with speed whiskers and one is seen in this condition at Birmingham Snow Hill in May 1959.

Significant improvements were made to suburban services in South Wales from January 1958 when the region received a substantial allocation of Class 116s. These were from the first batch built and had the four marker-light layout as can be seen on this unit at Blaenavon High Level. Services operated included Cardiff to Barry and what are now known as the Valley Lines, a route with which the class was to become synonymous in future years, lasting there until 1992. Three distinct batches of these units were constructed and there were subtle differences between these, not least in the treatment of the front ends, and the number of marker lights and route indicators provided. Although the new units were a considerable improvement on the steam-hauled suburban services which had preceded them they contrasted with the run-down state of the stations, many of which had had little or no improvement since the early days of the Great Western Railway.

Opposite top: Even though the plain livery of the Class 116 was austere it was quite pleasing when clean as can be seen here in this shot of a brand-new unit stabled at Birmingham Snow Hill. The driver appears to be applying the handbrake in the leading cab prior to leaving his unit, which is so new it still has the white lining round the wheels. The first two batches of Class 116 had only one wiper arm fitted but the last batch had wipers fitted at each side, much to the relief of both the secondmen and the public who then as now relished the view ahead through the driver's cab! The railway round Snow Hill in Birmingham has changed dramatically since this photograph was taken as the original station was abandoned and then demolished, before being reopened later in completely different form underneath a crop of modern buildings. This shot appears to be close to the point at which the city's urban motorway now buries underneath the line.

Opposite bottom: The West of England also benefitted from the allocation of suburban units, with Bristol getting its first examples in October 1958. From time to time these travelled more widely and often turned up on the Devon and Cornwall branch line network. For these duties sets were frequently shortened from three to two cars as can be seen here at Newquay in April 1965 where a Class 116, with its Driving Motor Second leading, awaits departure on a service to Par. Newquay's station was opened in 1865 and reached its largest form in 1938, when excursion trains regularly reached there from destinations such as London. Today it has only one platform and the original awnings have long gone, to be replaced with a modern wave-shaped structure.

Above: A Bridgend-bound suburban three-car Class 116 unit draws into Barry station on May 23 1964. This is from the final batch of these trains as it has two sets of windscreen wipers and a central route indicator. British Railways soon realised that they had made a mistake when specifying suburban units and work was put in hand to add corridor connections and doorways between parts of the trains so that passengers could access different compartments and also the toilets, which were situated in the middle vehicle on sets which had them. The modifications also meant that the trains were suitable for 'conductor-guard' operation as the guard could now get to the passengers to collect the fares

Above: Blaenavon High Level Station opened in 1854, along with the rest of the line which ran along the valley floor from Blaenavon to Newport in South Wales. The station was closed on April 30 1962, a year before the Beeching report at a time of falling passenger numbers, but attempts had been made to revitalise traffic by the introduction of Class 116 suburban units, one of which is seen waiting to make its next journey away from the picturesque terminus. Today nothing remains and the site is covered with housing.

Opposite top: A little further along the line was Pontypool Crane Street which opened in 1852 and was the temporary terminus of the route while the extension to Blaenavon was built. This also closed in 1962 but part of the building lives on at the Pontypool and Blaenavon heritage railway. Unfortunately this scene, with its Class 116 suburban unit, has now been completely swept away and the site is now a supermarket car park. The 116 is from a later batch than the one in the previous photo, as it has only two marker lights and is equipped with a route indicator. The class was introduced to this route on December 2 1957, being the first service to be dieselised in the area.

Opposite bottom; Despite being designated as suburban units, DMUs to this layout actually worked some routes which would be considered to be long distance today. South Wales-based units could be found working to places as far afield as Taunton in Somerset and it is one of these which is seen running through the majestic Sydney Gardens in Bath on July 8 1961. Drivers were instructed in the early days to keep the cab blinds in the up position when running in daylight so that passengers could see the view ahead.

Above: The Beeching Axe brought to an end services on many lines, some of which still carried substantial traffic and warranted the use of suburban-style DMUs. One of these was the former Great Central main line on which four-car Class 115 units were deployed, with London services terminating at Marylebone. These sets were regular performers also on the Chiltern lines for most of their lives, but later some were moved to Bletchley and Tyseley. One of these sets is seen running through Woodford Halse on the Great Central line, a location which once had a locomotive shed, wagon repair shops and an extensive marshalling yard, but which closed completely in 1966.

This page, top: The Class 116s were one of the classes selected for refurbishment, with the first being outshopped in the short-lived white with blue stripe livery in 1976. Prior to this they had carried plain blue livery. As might have been expected the white livery proved impractical and work soon started to paint the fleet in blue and grey. As sets were refurbished they also had their two-character route indicators or their centre marker lights removed, but some kept the light above the destination indicator. An immaculate three-car set is seen at Reading depot with Driving Motor Brake M50064 leading shortly after being refurbished.

This page, bottom: Towards the back end of their lives Bletchley-allocated Class 117s were reduced from three to two cars and were allocated set numbers in the L700-724 range for identification purposes. These survivors were painted in full Network Rail Southeast livery which looked somewhat strange when applied to a first-generation DMU. With Clapham Junction its eventual destination Driving Motor Brake 51359 trundles along near Kensington Olympia station on August 19 1996. Only two years after the date of this photograph suburban DMUs were to be no more, with all having been replaced by more modern types of unit.

Opposite bottom: Initially the 20 three-car Class 125 units were deployed on Lea Valley services on the GE main line from Liverpool Street, but could be seen as far out as Southminster and on some of the branches in Essex. Once this route was electrified, they were transferred to Finsbury Park and used for peak hour only suburban services. However, due to their use of Rolls-Royce engines and hydraulic transmission they were not particularly successful and thus were slated for early withdrawal. All were removed from service over the winter of 1976-77. On April 19 1976 and in plain blue livery two of these sets run into Dalston Junction, a station in North London which is now served by trains from London Overground.

Chapter Eight
Single Cars

In some cases traffic requirements could be satisfied by the use of a single-car vehicle. As a result a number of different types of both passenger and parcels cars were constructed.

Although some were allocated to branch line work, others could be seen in urban areas where they were sometimes used to strengthen other sets or worked in multiple.

Above; Two single car versions of the original Derby Lightweight were constructed for use on the Buckingham to Banbury route. Plans had been proposed for the use of railbuses for this but the London Midland Region's management had other ideas. Two Driving Motor Brake seconds, which were originally intended for the Manchester part one dieselisation scheme were altered while in production and emerged in August 1956 with a cab at each end. There were differences between the two relating to the size of the guard's van, and though the internal layout was soon altered so that both matched, they had a slightly different side window layout throughout their lives. Here M79901 calls at Radclive Halt with a train bound for Bletchley.

Opposite top: Only one of the two units was used in traffic each day but there were occasions when they were coupled together and worked in multiple. Loadings improved by much more than had been hoped but even within three months of the Lightweight's introduction management had concluded that the line could never make enough money to pay its way. By June 1958 proposals were in hand to close the route, and this was achieved by 1960. Although there were plans to deploy the two single cars elsewhere only M79900 was to survive, and this in departmental service, while its sister was broken up. In better times M79901 is seen at Buckingham station awaiting its next turn of duty.

Above: The Gloucester Railway Carriage and Wagon Company built 20 single cars for use by the Western Region in the London and Birmingham areas. These were designed by Derby works and were a double-ended version of the Class 116, complete with suburban layout. Fitted with AEC engines and standard 'blue square' wiring these vehicles could work with most other classes ordered in the late 1950s. Initially these were used on lightly-loaded routes including the infamous Stourbridge Town to Stourbridge Junction branch and covered many services in the West of England, such as in Devon and Cornwall. Later designated as Class 122 the first of these cars appeared in April 1958. First-built W55000 is seen at Swindon works in almost new condition in that year.

Above: Following on from the Class 122s Pressed Steel of Linwood in Scotland were contracted to build an additional batch of basically similar vehicles, also for the Western Region. This time 16 power cars were built with these set to work around Bristol, Plymouth and Reading, some taking over duties from the former Great Western railcars. The Pressed Steel vehicles, which became Class 121, could be identified by the fact that they were fitted with a four-character headcode box rather than a route indicator and initially had a slightly different arrangement of exhaust pipes at the end. Some of these versatile units found work in the West of Wales and, on May 17 1964, one of them, W55026, is seen stabled at Neyland, a station that was once intended to serve a trans-Atlantic port but which ended up as a remote outpost due to the development of Fishguard. The station closed completely a month after the photograph was taken.

Opposite top: When the single cars were built consideration was given as to how traffic requirements could best be dealt with on busy days and in consequence some single-ended Driving Trailers were built which could work with them. Each of the two manufacturers supplied ten trailers each and these were to be the only suburban-style driving vehicles which did not have engines underneath them. Corridor connections were not provided because the vehicles would have to be coupled to a driving end of the power car, whichever end they were attached at. These trailers spent a great deal of time parked up and were often only used one or two days a week. Bourne End station is on the Marlow Branch between Maidenhead and Marlow and its branch services are often referred to as the 'Marlow Donkey'. Here the 'Donkey' led by one of the Class 121 Driving Trailers pauses at the station before resuming its journey.

Opposite bottom: Because DMUs had limited parcels accommodation compared with steam trains a number of single-car parcels vehicles were ordered, which could either work on their own or be attached to passenger trains. Cravens of Sheffield built three cars in 1958 which were intended for use in West Cumberland and were therefore fitted with 'yellow diamond' electrics so that they could work with the Derby Lightweights. However, only M55997 reached its intended area and the other two were found work in the Midlands, where their non-standard set-up soon became a problem. All were out of service by 1973, although one survived for a while as a departmental vehicle. M55997 was captured at Whitehaven on August 19 1959 performing its usual Carlisle-Whitehaven daily parcels run.

Single Cars

British Railways Modernisation-Era DMUs

Opposite top: Ten more diesel parcels units were ordered by British Railways in 1958 but these differed from the previously-delivered Cravens vehicles in that they were heavier and longer and were also equipped with Albion 230hp engines so that they could be used to haul tail loads of parcels vehicles or goods wagons. These vehicles were built by the Gloucester Railway Carriage and Wagon Works and were to a length of 62ft, the same as the suburban DMU coaches, rather than the shorter length used for the Cravens. Three pairs of sliding doors were fitted on each side and the vehicles, which were to become Class 128, were wired to the Blue Square standard so that they were capable of being worked in multiple with most of the rest of the DMU fleet. The first four vehicles were delivered to the Midland Region, and initially allocated to Cricklewood, and these had a three-window cab front with a four-character route indicator located directly beneath it.

Opposite bottom; The final six Class 128s which followed were for the Western Region, but these differed in that they were fitted with end gangways, meaning that the route indicator had to be split each side. The first two units were allocated to Southall while the rest were all soon allocated to the Birmingham area. Strangely the bulk of the Western Region vehicles soon found themselves allocated to the Midland Region when Tyseley depot was itself transferred. Many of the duties undertaken by the London-based examples had been originally allocated to the former Great Western parcels cars, with most of the class spending a great deal of time hauling one or more bogie parcels vehicles for additional capacity. Here W55992 is pictured at Southall as it works a parcels service to Paddington on August 6 1960.

Above: Unusually for DMU vehicles the Class 128s were often employed to shunt short rakes of parcels or goods stock, with many of their duties in the London area being of the short-haul type. A little later in their careers some were paired up with former Class 116 vehicles which had been stripped out for parcels use as an alternative way to provide extra capacity but they were also sometimes used in pairs. The Class 128s were very stylish vehicles, despite being designed for a mundane use, with W55991 ably exhibiting this in this view at Westbourne Bridge taken on September 10 1960.

Above: It was typical of the British Railways of the period that the single cars were allowed to soon become run-down and dirty, negating the purpose for which they were introduced, namely attracting additional passengers. Discarded materials surround Gloucester Railway Carriage and Wagon-built Class 122 M55007 as it stands on Worcester shed on June 26 1964, unbelievably the vehicle was only about five years old when this photograph was taken. The shed itself was only to last for a further year as it was closed as the steam fleet in the region was run down. All the single cars became known as 'bubble cars' during the 1960s in homage to the little three-wheeled cars that were popular at the time, and many have survived into preservation and can be seen at several of our heritage railways today.

Opposite top: One duty which was exclusively reserved for the single cars for many years was that on the short branchline between Stourbridge Junction and Stourbridge Town in the West Midlands. This twisty 0.8 mile long branch descended towards Stourbridge on a keen gradient, which led to at least two of the single cars overshooting the terminus station and coming to rest overhanging the road at the end of the line. As a result of this and other incidents additional instrumentation was fitted in the 'bubble car's' cab so that the driver could easily detect if there was any reduction in brake performance. One of the Gloucester-built Class 122s stands at the end of the line at Stourbridge Town on September 9 1972. This station was demolished in 1979 when the line was cut back by a few yards to allow for the building of a new bus station.

Opposite bottom: Both the Pressed Steel and the Gloucester-built single cars lost their green livery in favour of first blue and then blue and grey, with this scheme being seen on W55029 which is operating the Windsor branch service from Slough station. It is attached to one of the Driving Trailers, which still retains its blue livery. Many units later gained headlights and there were also several different patterns of exhausts fitted. This unit has had a modification to the heating system as can be seen by the additional grille near the guard's door. It still exists today, at the Rushden Transport Museum, having been preserved after departmental use and is undergoing a long restoration to passenger condition using components retrieved from a Class 117 which was being broken up.

Single Cars

Opposite top: In later life most of the Class 128 parcels cars were allocated either to Newton Heath in Manchester or to Chester depots, with the remaining two Western Region units still at Reading. Duties for the North west-allocated sets included along the North Wales coast and also to and from the Midlands. Interestingly, when there were issues with the Barmouth Bridge, which prevented the use of locomotives across it, Class 128s were used as the motive power for permanent way trains and could be seen hauling ballast wagons as well as other track materials along the Cambrian coast. At this time Manchester Victoria almost always played host to one or other of these units, which by this time had had their corridor connections removed and plated over. M55993 is seen in one of the bays which today form part of the Metrolink tram station.

Opposite bottom: Everything in this scene has now gone. The old Manchester Victoria station was swept away and the new one is now buried under the arena, Gloucester unit M55994 moved to Tyseley in 1985 before receiving a coat of Royal Mail red and then lasted for a further five years before being withdrawn. By this time the survivors had been fitted with Leyland TL11 engines, similar to those used on the 'Pacers'. Behind the Class 128 is a Class 31 diesel, more than likely one of those allocated to the station as a banker for heavy trains which needed to proceed up to Miles Platting. M55994 was taken to Derby for parts recovery and then remarkably towed to Inverness for similar work which is not thought to have been completed before the vehicle was cut up for scrap.

Above: M79900, one of the original pair of single cars built for the London Midland Region had a charmed life following its withdrawal from passenger service. Whilst its sister went for scrap this car became a route learner on the Eastern Region based at York before passing in 1974 to the Railway Technical Centre at Derby. There it was renumbered RDB975010 and travelled widely in connection with radio tests, as seen here on January 16 1986 when it reached Dingwall in the Scottish Highlands. When repainted in RTC red and blue livery the vehicle was named 'Test Car Iris', a name that has stuck with it right to the present day. Withdrawn from RTC service in June 1999 'Iris' was restored to passenger configuration at the Midland Railway– at Butterley and can now be found at work at the Ecclesbourne Valley Railway.

Left: The Scottish Region converted three of the Class 122s into single car parcels vehicles in the late-1960s, with the vehicles being allocated to Leith Central from where they worked the Edinburgh to Stirling and Dundee route, normally coupled to service trains. These conversions saw all the seats and interior fittings removed, as were the door handles and grab rails, as can be seen in this view of Sc55015 at Stirling station. Other cars were converted into route learners or departmental vehicles as the branch lines for which they had been intended were closed down under the Beeching axe.

Bottom: One of those converted to departmental use was 55008 which became TDB975309 and which was used as a route learner between 1974 and 1982. Allocated originally to Tyseley it moved to York in 1972 and became a departmental vehicle a couple of years later, at one point receiving a rather peculiar matt olive livery. As can be seen, tiered seating had been added at both ends to enable a better view for those learning the route and the destination indicator had been removed from the roof dome. Later in its career the car also lost its two-character route indicator as well, and had a gas cylinder box added underneath to power cooking facilities inside.

Chapter Nine

Accidents and Mishaps

With over 4,500 units built during the Modernisation Plan era, the type came to dominate local services for almost three decades. Inevitably there were many mishaps and accidents, which have mostly gone unrecorded.

However, accidents were always of interest to the authorities, the local press and to enthusiasts and this has resulted in a selection of photographs surviving.

Top: On August 10 1961 two four-car Class 101 units left Leeds City station on their way to Scarborough and shortly after their journey commenced they were sideswiped by 'Peak' class locomotive D105 which had failed to stop at a signal and which then pushed the leading DMU car, E51440, over onto its side. The accident took place on the viaduct outside the station and materials from the parapet wall were cascaded down into the streets and yards below. The second coach in the rake, a centre trailer, also fell over onto its side. Unfortunately, one person was killed in the incident and another two were injured.

Bottom: Another accident where a DMU was struck by a train which had over-run signals was at York on June 15 1965. Five empty coaches were being propelled by a Class 25 from the station to the carriage sidings when they struck an eight-car DMU set, which was travelling from Scarborough to Leeds. The empty stock had run through three red signals, and although it hit the DMU at low speed considerable damage was caused, with 15 people, including three railwaymen also suffering injury. The leading DMU car, Metro-Cammell Class 101 E50236, was seriously damaged in the incident.

Above: A year prior to the York accident a serious incident occurred at Bradford Exchange station when the driver of a Manchester Victoria to Leeds stopping train was taken ill as the unit approached Bradford Exchange station, which is at the bottom of a steep hill. The train ran past a series of signals at danger before running into the station's platform four and colliding head on with the standing steam locomotive of a mail train. The collision, which occurred at about 50mph, caused the DMU to ride over the steam engine, killing the driver and another railwayman who was travelling passenger. A passenger was to die later in hospital, while many others, realising the excess speed of the train, had run to the rear coach to escape the results of the impact. The leading car was Class 108 Driving Motor Brake M51944 which had to be written off as a result of the collision.

Opposite top: York-allocated 'B1' 4-6-0 61086 has come into contact with a Cravens DMU, which has been turned over onto its side in an incident of which no details appear to have been recorded. The 'B1', which is hauling a freight train, appears to have sideswiped the unit, causing it to fall over, and in the process has detached the front bogie. DMUs were very prone to turning over when involved in this type of incident, which was quite common in the days before Automatic Warning equipment was fitted to all traction units.

Opposite bottom: Another shot which looks as though it has come from the North east, given the design of the footbridge which appears to be of North Eastern Railway origin, shows a steam crane hard at work lifting a Class 104 Birmingham RCW unit after it has come to grief by overrunning a set of buffers. Crane lifts of this kind could rarely be carried out without causing further damage to the vehicles being recovered and, as can be seen here, this often involved bodyside dents where the crane slings had come into contact with the bodywork.

Bogies and Bufferstops: In the 1950s and 1960s railway accidents were far more common than they are today. Low speed derailments and collisions were common, with DMUs being particularly prone to extensive damage, even in the most minor derailments.

Opposite top: Many minor accidents were caused when routes were incorrectly set or where points were moved under vehicles as they went over them. This Metro-Cammell Class 101 bound for Bradford Exchange seems to have split the points, resulting in its front bogie rotating round and becoming jammed in the tracks. Although the vehicle appears to be little damaged it will in fact have suffered a great deal around the bogie pivot area. The breakdown train has just pulled up on the left of the picture while the suitably-hatted manager inspects the damage.

Opposite bottom: Another shot of the unfortunate E50236, which was the same vehicle involved in the 1965 York accident described earlier and which seems to have got itself into another spot of bother. This time it has collided heavily with the buffer stops at what looks like a pre-rebuilding Leeds City station. The buffer stops have risen up and have broken the cab windscreens but otherwise the unit seems to have come out reasonably unscathed. This car was reported as being withdrawn as a result of damage sustained at York so this incident must have occurred before that.

Above: This Hull-bound Class 104 appears to have suffered a similar fate and is off all wheels with the breakdown crane in attendance. Here the lift is being attempted by slinging under the front bufferbeam, rather than by using the side lifting points and the plan would normally be to lift the front of the unit and then to slew it to one side so that it could be re-railed more or less in a straight line. The second coach of this consist is one of the relatively rare centre brake vehicles, only 26 were built, and interestingly a handbrake was fitted in the guard's compartment, a feature that was not replicated where the brake van was part of a power car.

Chapter Ten
Depots and Sidings

The introduction of the first-generation units did not only mean that new trains were provided, but also that new depot and maintenance facilities were required. At first these were quite primitive but in time purpose-built sheds were built, which did a great deal to improve both the availability and reliability of the new DMUs. Because of the lack of access to these depots photographs are relatively rare but some do exist, many of them coming from official railway or newspaper sources.

The first depot to have an allocation of DMUs was Bradford (Hammerton Street) which received an allocation in 1954. The site was formerly known as Bowling shed and for a while DMUs shared facilities with steam traction. The main running shed was a whitewashed building which had lost its roof and as might be imagined cleanliness was almost non-existent, a factor which contributed to poor availability from the DMU fleet. After a while steam was banished, clean areas established and some rebuilding took place. Amongst the new equipment installed was a carriage washer which was designed to clean a complete DMU in a matter of minutes. One of the first series of 'Derby Lightweights' can be seen making good use of the wash in what appears to be a publicity picture.

Right: Over a period of five years or so British Railways made a considerable investment in diesel facilities at depots, in some cases by modifying older buildings and on others in building from scratch. Here a Metro-Cammell DMU is receiving fitters' attention in a modified steam shed, which had had full-length pit lighting provided as well as a good clean up. The arrival of the diesels gave rise to a steep learning curve for fitters, many of whom found it difficult to cope with the attention to detail which diesels required. There was also an increased demand for ancillary trades such as electricians, as much of the operation of a DMU took place electrically.

Bottom: It was soon realised that there was a considerable advantage in having a sunken area each side of the rails as this allowed work to take place on the brakes and external mechanical and electrical parts. This led to many depots being built with a sunken floor, having the rails raised slightly to allow easy access all round the unit. Here Edinburgh-Glasgow Driving Motor Brake Sc79016 has been split from its sister vehicles for attention while full sets await their next duty on the roads behind. Although not recorded as such this image seems to have been taken in Leith Central depot.

Opposite top: Dundee West shed opened in 1885 and closed to steam in 1958. Later it reopened as a diesel depot, lasting for another 20 years. The shed received many Metro-Cammell vehicles including a series of two and three-car sets which mainly worked to Edinburgh and Glasgow. Two of these are seen in ex-works condition in storage in the shed and awaiting their first turn of duty, these are presumably from the 1958 batch of power-trailers which were followed in 1959 by some three -car sets which had two powered vehicles.

Opposite bottom: At many sheds attempts were made to keep as many of the in-service sets under cover as possible. Appearing to have been taken at booking-on time this shot shows North Eastern Region-allocated Class 108 Driving Motor Composite NE50639 nicely under cover. This vehicle was part of a three-car set delivered in 1958 and which was allocated to Hull Botanic Gardens, where this photo was taken. It later moved on to South Gosforth depot in Newcastle, and also to Darlington.

Right: Every attempt was made to promote the modern image promoted by the arrival of the diesels and whenever depot open days or exhibitions were held a unit was always provided. This is the case here where an early Derby Lightweight from the Leeds batch can be seen on show at an unrecorded location, which may well be the roundhouse at Neville Hill depot. Then as now trains were a constant object of interest for small children.

Below: Many sets were stored for some months before being brought into service, with one of the locations used for this being Warwick Milverton shed which played host to a number of new Class 108s for a time in 1959. Taken on March 28 of that year this shot shows the six sets that were stored there, which were all power-trailers and consisted of Driving Motor Brakes M50947-52 and Driving Trailers M56230-35. Others from this batch were stored at many other depots until enough were available to turn entire timetables over to diesel operation.

Right: Dundee West shed plays host to withdrawn and heavily stripped Derby Lightweight Driving Trailer E79252, which was originally delivered to Norwich depot in East Anglia in 1955. The Scottish Region took some sets from Bletchley and Norwich in 1966 with this coach being one of those transferred to Leith. All were withdrawn by June 1967 but 79252 was taken into departmental service and nominally renumbered 975014, with the intention that it should be used as staff accommodation. This was one of two conversions of this nature carried out with the final one not being scrapped until 1982.

Bottom: Most of the first-generation DMU fleet met an ignominious end at the hands of the scrapman, some many years before they were truly life-expired. Here a Derby Lightweight is being cut up while behind it there are various examples of Type 1 locomotives that are also meeting a premature end. Although units were being scrapped in 1964, it was to be 2017 before the last one was taken out of service, a truly remarkable number of years for any design concept to remain in service. Fortunately, more than 400 individual DMU cars from the first generation remain on our heritage railways and today the scrapman has moved on to units built more than 30 years after these popular vehicles.